Math & Movement
training manual for elementary schools

by Suzy Koontz

With Laura Gates-Lupton

Illustrated by Chad Hovey

This book is dedicated to Margaret Steinacher, first grade teacher *par excellence*, to my husband, Bruce and to my children, Elizabeth, Emily, Jessica and Sarah. SDK

Copyright 2010 by Suzanne Kuntz

Math and Movement Training Manual for Elementary Schools

ISBN 978-0-9815146-6-6

Printed in the United States of America

Book design by Chad Hovey

For further information visit http://www.mathandmovement.com

Table of Contents

Introduction 5
Active Math—Whisper/Loud 17
Active Math—Skip Counting Movements 59
Sit-Down Math 85
Tapping at the Table 103
Hallway Math 115
Math and Yoga 125
Activities for the *Math&Movement* Floor Mats and Banners 129
Integrating *Math&Movement* Into the Day 147
Extending the *Math&Movement* Program 163
Conclusion 169

Introduction

Do your students have so much energy that it's hard for them to sit still? Children are naturally active learners, using their bodies along with their minds to practice and acquire new skills. *Math&Movement* is a supplemental program that harnesses children's natural desire to move and gives children more opportunities to practice math skills until mastery is achieved.

I am the mother of four children. My second child needs to move. Sitting still for more than a few minutes has never been part of her game plan. Sitting down to learn math was definitely out of the question. Prior to having children, I worked for many years to understand math concepts and developed a strong passion for facilitating the process of learning math. I held opinions about the value that competence in math offered children. I felt desperate to find enjoyable methods for her to learn math.

One sunny afternoon, while we soaked in the much needed sunshine in Upstate New York, we sat outside working on skip counting. It was slow going and not very much fun until she had an inspiration. She climbed on the trampoline and began to jump while simultaneously practicing her skip counting. The results were amazing! She began to learn so quickly that we decided to make jumping and skip counting a regular part of her "learn to multiply" routine. This resulted in her mastering multiplication in record time while enjoying the process immensely — my first glimpse at the magic of movement.

After further study, I learned that movement is not magical in itself but rather that research has found a correlation between movement and enhanced learning! Multiple studies have confirmed that exercise stimulates brain growth. For example, according to Carla Hannaford, PhD, author of *Smart Moves, Why Learning is Not All in Your Head* (Great River Books, 2005), "The more closely we consider the elaborate interplay of brain and body, the more clearly one compelling theme emerges: movement is essential to learning. ... Movement awakens and activates our mental capacities. Movement integrates and anchors new information and experience into our neural networks. Moving while learning increases learning."

Eric Jensen writes "Research suggests that physical activity benefits learning. Movement increases heart rate and circulation, enhances spatial learning, provides a break from learning, allows cognitive maturation, stimulates the release of beneficial chemicals, counteracts excessive sitting, and affirms the value of implicit learning." *Moving With the Brain in Mind,* Educational Leadership, v58 n3 p34-37 Nov 2000.

Introduction

Dr. John Ratey, author of *Spark: The Revolutionary New Science of Exercise and the Brain* states "I cannot underestimate how important regular exercise is in improving the function and performance of the brain. Exercise stimulates our gray matter to produce 'Miracle-Gro' for the brain." This refers to the brain chemical BDNF (brain-derived-neurotropic factor). Exercise stimulates the brain to produce extra BDNF which is used to enhance the development of new neurons (and their connections).

The *Math&Movement* program is based on research that suggests that moving during learning facilitates muscle memory, an important factor with younger children whose abstract thinking skills are not fully developed. It is also based on research suggesting that cross-body movements integrate the left and right hemisphere of the brain. Cross-body movements are when the left arms or legs cross over to the right side of the body or right arms or legs cross over to the left side of the body. These movements wake up a "sleepy" brain and help to cement newly learned material in the memory.

We Have a Math Crisis

Americans are lagging behind other countries in math. The PISA (Programme for International Student Assessment) evaluation of 15-year-old students' math scores found that Americans rank 24 out of 29 industrialized nations. America sadly ranks behind 23 countries including Canada, Australia, New Zealand and Spain. In addition, the level of obesity in children is at an all time high. The *Math&Movement* program contributes to the solution of these problems by combating obesity while simultaneously improving math skills and retention.

What are the ramifications of math illiteracy? Recently I visited the space center at Cape Canaveral. I had the pleasure of listening to the story of an astronaut's journey into space. At the conclusion of his talk he shared exciting plans for the future of space travel, colonies on the moon and Mars and future exploration of the universe. However, he said, "This may not be possible because we do not have enough American students who are competent in math." In the US, there are at most 5,000 students studying aerospace engineering contrasted with one Chinese university (out of many) that has over 20,000 students eager to be hired into the space industry. Other professions need math-competent individuals as well. The following fields all depend on math.

Medical schools need students competent in math
Dentistry, veterinary medicine and other medical fields—all depend on math
Engineers build our world and need math
The financial industry needs math!

There are many fields open to our graduates who are competent in math and many foreign graduates ready to fill the vacancies.

Math is Possible for Everyone!

Many students are giving up on math at a relatively young age; it doesn't have to be this way. *Math&Movement* gives students a successful experience with math before they develop the "I can't do math attitude." It gives them the confidence to take mathematical risks.

Math phobia is rampant among adults with over 60% of Americans affected. Sheila Tobias, author of *Overcoming Math Anxiety* and *Succeed with Math* believes that math anxiety begins by feeling uncomfortable with math in elementary school. *Math&Movement* short circuits math-phobia by increasing student's math ability and math confidence. Commencing *Math&Movement* activities at a young age jumpstarts a child's positive attitude toward math. *Math&Movement* is a movement-based program. The activities catch children when they are still willing to give math a try.

Math is another language. Children are receptive to languages. I believe that unless we include more math for children in pre-school through grade four, we are missing a crucial window of opportunity in the lives of our young children. Because *Math&Movement* allows children to learn through movement and visually pleasing floor mats, math concepts become accessible to young children. The depth of understanding acquired in play-like activities will serve as a base for later construction of more advanced concepts. The intent of *Math&Movement* is not to create a push-down curriculum but rather to allow children to experience math success before they have developed any "math phobias," or any hint that math is hard!

Background Information on *Math&Movement*

Math&Movement began as a pilot study in a first grade classroom. My goal was to determine if the techniques used in my book for parents, *Multiply With Me, Learning to Multiply Can Be Fun,* were applicable in the classroom. I had studied the Brain-Gym® model previously and was thrilled to learn that the teacher incorporated Brain-Gym® into her classroom. My goal in designing the movements was to use cross-body movements and the whisper/loud counting technique from my book.

Designing movements that kids could actually remember and repeat without confusion was troublesome until I had a break-through in my thought process. As long as children did movements that used different parts of their body—such as toes, then knees, then hips and shoulders, the children could remember the movements.

Benefits of *Math&Movement*

It is generally understood in the United States today that many school children are far less able in mathematics than is desirable and that many children are so lacking in exercise that there are serious detrimental effects to health and learning. At the same time, it is well-understood that teachers are so overburdened with heavy curriculum demands that adding special new programs is problematic. I am proposing ways of addressing these concerns within the existing programs through the incorporation of the practices and materials of *Math&Movement*.

Math&Movement is a kinesthetic, multi-sensory approach to teaching math that incorporates physical exercise. Many studies suggest that exercise stimulates learning. At-risk students often benefit from kinesthetic approaches to learning. *Math&Movement* offers an alternative approach to learning designed to "close the gap" and give every child the opportunity to become competent and confident in their math abilities.

Why Combine Movement and Learning?

Students feel better and have an increased ability to focus when movement is incorporated into their daily routine. Research suggests that it is prudent to redesign learning environments to incorporate the use of movement at regular intervals.

The Case for Adopting *Math&Movement* in Your Classroom and School

Anyone familiar with the habits of children knows that children love to move. Movement is pleasurable and natural to children. It is logical to combine movement with learning, to offer pleasurable activities for children, to harness their love of movement and use it for enhanced learning. In addition, movement is healthy for children. Children who engage in physical activity are healthier and more alert. In addition, Math&Movement:

Strengthens numeracy and literacy

One-to-one correspondence, which is defined as the ability to link a number name with one and only one object, is fundamental in both numeracy and literacy. The inclusion of additional practice allows children to become grounded in one-to-one correspondence thus laying a sturdy foundation for learning additional math concepts. In addition, beginning readers benefit from continual practice with one-to-one-correspondence.

When children begin the *Math&Movement* exercises, they may not be able to coordinate their movements to the recitations of counting. However, as they imitate the leader and their classmates, and continue to engage in the exercises, they gradually become able to understand the concept of one-to-one correspondence.

Is aligned with the NCTM Principles and Standards

The activities are designed for pre-K through grade 5. The primary focus of the *Math&Movement* program is in the area of Numbers and Operations as designated in the statement of Principles and Standards identified by the National Council of Teachers of Mathematics (1989).

Supplements existing curricula

One-to-one correspondence, addition, subtraction, multiplication, division, fractions, least common denominators, greatest common factors and factoring are key components of all math curriculums. More practice time is necessary to ensure competence in basic arithmetic. *Math&Movement* activities are designed to fit into transitional times, therefore not taking time away from other core subjects.

After children reach closure in their math facts, they have an increased ability to understand word problems, estimation, and are able to retain more content from the regular math curriculum.

Easily fits into the school day

The *Math&Movement* program makes it possible to create learning opportunities during non-classroom time such as while standing in line, walking in hallways, transitioning between activities, as well as in physical education classes, after-school programs and school vacations. The possibilities for including *Math&Movement* activities during a child's day are endless.

Allows children to exceed state standards

Children who are introduced to *Math&Movement* activities become confident in their math basics thus allowing them to learn addition, subtraction, multiplication, division, fractions, decimals, percents, factoring and algebra at an earlier age.

In many first grade classes children have loved learning to multiply! In one Kindergarten class, the children learned to skip count by twos so quickly that we introduced skip counting by threes. In a third grade class, the children loved learning algebra and begged for more and more algebra worksheets. First graders learning multiplication are generally two-years ahead of the traditional age for learning multiplication, greatly exceeding state expectations.

Integrates core subjects

It is often easier to integrate language arts with history and science than to integrate math. One has to be more creative to integrate math. *Math&Movement* integrates easily with PE. Children find it exceedingly pleasurable to count as they engage in their many physical activities.

Engages all learners

How often do you see children begging to do just one more math activity? With *Math&Movement*, children so enjoy designing math movements and performing them that they forget they are practicing math.

In one first grade classroom, one of the boys with a disability spent the entire program seemingly disengaged. When we began the lesson for skip counting by sixes, he surprised me by coming right up to me and announcing that he had an activity. He demonstrated it, and it indeed used the multiples of six. Furthermore, it was a clever activity. He must have thought about this beforehand!

In a third grade class, I was amazed at how quickly the students discovered their own cleverness for inventing *Math&Movement* activities! They begged to pretend they were chipmunks, bunnies, or disco dancers. Who would ever think that a movement needed to include a nice, solid lick of your arm? One first grader insisted that we were tigers and that licking was an essential component of the movement! We named the movement "Tiger Lick!"

Makes math imaginative and creative

Memories of math class for most include the boring drill and repetition of math basics. Unfortunately the repetition is necessary just as it is for beginning readers, but *Math&Movement* adds imagination and creativity to the necessary practice. Once you introduce your students to the movements included in this book, encourage them to create and lead their own movement activities. This allows math practice to become an opportunity for imagination, creativity, cooperation, assertion, responsibility, self-control and leadership.

Is classroom-tested

Four independent elementary schools and over 300 children have participated in activities from the *Math&Movement* program. The cleverest activities included in this training manual were designed by children for children. The children consistently have

the same positive reaction to the *Math&Movement* activities! One boy said, "The movements are my favorite part of math class--I love this!"

Is research-based

Math&Movement incorporates physical exercise, stretching, cross-body movements and yoga. I have also drawn from the work of Paul E. Dennison (brain-gym), Eric Jensen, Howard Gardner, John Ratey and the Waldorf and Montessori teaching philosophies.

In addition, a Northeast Elementary school pilot study, showed a five-fold increase in learning multiples, and first graders learned to multiply and expressed delight in the acquisition of math skills and showed that children as young as six could master multiplication. The ten-week pilot study considered 21 first graders' (ten girls and eleven boys) abilities in skip counting, addition skills, multiplication skills, one-to-one-correspondence, enthusiasm in math, confidence in math and math ability before and after introducing movement activities designed to enhance learning to skip count and multiply.

Of the 21 students, there were seven Asians or Asian-Americans, two African-Americans, and twelve Caucasians. In less than 18 hours of instruction, the first graders learned multiplication up to ten times ten, as well as the basic concepts of square numbers, square roots, fractions, decimals and percents.

Supports equity

All students participate simultaneously in the *Math&Movement* activities. Children from all backgrounds and socio-economic levels can benefit from *Math&Movement* activities, especially those who are kinesthetic learners. Experts believe that a high percentage of children in poverty are kinesthetic learners. *Math&Movement* activities can help eliminate race and class as predictors of success.

In one classroom, three of the students were identified as needing intervention services. These students participated happily along with the other students in the class. The math specialist reported a noticeable increase in math ability and confidence.

After a *Math&Movement* workshop, teachers who attended wrote to me:

I found the workshop very inspiring. I have been doing a session of Math&Movement every day with my students and they are enjoying it! I am sure it will help with their facts.

So far today I have worked with a whole class and a small group and they loved it! One

Introduction

4th grader, who does not know her facts, was able to skip count by 6's to 36 after doing the Jaguar Tummy Rub and skip hopping for 15 minutes! Thank you so much!

Reinforces math learning while adding additional PE minutes

Your school may be in need of adding additional PE minutes to the schedule. M&M can count. The activities in the Active Math section are designed to give children aerobic exercise. These activities may meet the requirements for additional physical education minutes depending on state regulations. Many state regulations encourage integrating learning core subjects with physical activity. Most states have a procedure to follow. Check your state's website for details.

Builds basic multiplication skill

Generic multiplication skill is at the core of most mathematical thinking and ability. Skip counting skill will enhance multiplication skill and understanding. Rote learning of abstract concepts has low retention value (especially in young children). Mathematical concepts not fully grasped continue to plague the learning of later, more comprehensive mathematical concepts.

Facilitates learning more advanced math concepts

Knowing skip counting greatly facilitates the process of learning multiplication, division, fractions, decimals, percents, factoring and algebra. See Implementation of *Math&Movement* for a step-by-step approach on how to use skip counting to reach closure with multiplication.

Is developmentally appropriate for pre-school children

The importance of imaginative play must be recognized. *Math&Movement* must never be considered a push-down curriculum. Movement is natural and pleasurable for children. *Math&Movement* activities are enjoyable because they see the activities as game. In addition, movement while learning facilitates muscle memory, an important factor with younger children whose abstract thinking skills are not fully developed. Also, the brain chemical dopamine, released when children are enjoying themselves, enhances learning, retention of knowledge and the transfer of learning.

The magic of the *Math&Movement* program is that children become so engaged that they forget they are practicing math. Children are encouraged to use their creative imagination to develop and participate in new movements. In a class full of eighteen or more children, with eighteen unique ideas, your students will receive an abundant amount of math practice.

Introduction

While visiting a class with young children, I asked my favorite question: who has an idea? Hands immediately popped up all over the room. Their ideas were unique, inspiring and significantly more interesting than the ones I had thought of! To be fair to everyone, each student had a chance to explain their idea for skip counting by twos and have the entire class participate in their idea for a movement. The end result—all the children learned to skip count by twos and felt proud of themselves for the acquisition of this skill.

The teacher benefits along with the students

Teachers who have used this program report that after engaging in the *Math&Movement* activities they felt mentally clear and energized.

The Structure of This Book

The book is organized into the following nine sections:

Active Math—Whisper/Loud Movements

Active Math: Whisper/Loud Movements are designed to give your students physical exercise while simultaneously enhancing math ability. Ninety student-generated, classroom-tested activities are included. There are ten movements per number from one through nine.

Active Math—Skip Counting Movements

Active Math: Skip Counting Movements are designed to provide additional physical exercise while learning the multiples. There are over one hundred student-generated, classroom-tested activities included in this section, at least four for each letter of the alphabet.

Sit-Down Math

Sit-Down Math activities are designed for quiet time and involve stretching. There are forty-three activities included.

Tapping at the Table

Tapping at the Table activities are designed to be used in between other activities, while students sit at their desks. There are thirty-six activities.

Hallway Math

Hallway Math activities are designed to be used walking in the hallway to and from lunch, PE, art, music, computer or library. There are twelve activities.

Introduction

Math and Yoga

Math and Yoga activities incorporate math practice into popular yoga moves. Nine activities are included. Math 'n the Five Tibetan Rites are included in this section.

Activities for the *Math&Movement* Floor Mats and Banners

This section includes over ninety activities that make the active learning with the floor mats and banners enjoyable. Activities are included for the Numberline 1-10 mat, the seven Numberline Hopping mats and the Add/Subtract mat (100 Number Grid).

Implementing *Math&Movement* into the Day

Included in this section are suggestions for times of the day to include *Math&Movement*, how skip counting transfers to multiplication and division mastery and how to enhance math on a day-to-day basis.

Extending the *Math&Movement* program

The Math Buddy Program, *Math&Movement* Night for Parents and Students, A-Penny-A-Problem math-a-thon, After School Math Immersion, Math 'n Tennis camp, Math 'n Summer Camp and Math Resource Centers are offered as suggestions to further enhance the math ability of your students.

In conclusion, the expected outcomes of adopting the *Math&Movement* program are enhanced learning, greater retention, and more enthusiasm of more children. Previously excluded children, like the kinesthetic learner, become engaged in mathematical learning and the increase in physical activity transfers to make learning other subjects easier for your students.

I hope that your students and you will enjoy these activities!

Suzy Koontz

Ithaca, New York
February, 2010

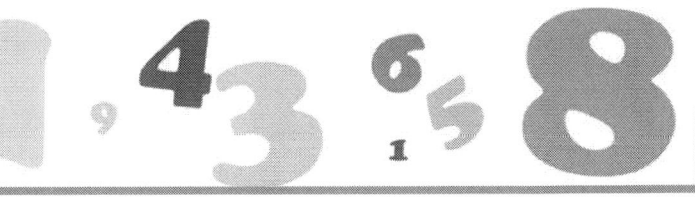

The Whisper/Loud Counting Technique

Many of the activities in this book use the whisper/loud technique, an effective way to reinforce the intervals in the number line for different multiples. This counting technique is as follows:

Children whisper (or mouth) the numbers that are not the multiples. When they say the multiple, they say the number louder or shout it. The following is an example of counting by threes using the whisper/loud counting method.

1 (whisper), *2* (whisper), *3* (LOUD)

4 (whisper), *5* (whisper), *6* (LOUD)

7 (whisper), *8* (whisper), *9* (LOUD)

10 (whisper), *11* (whisper), *12* (LOUD)

Active Math — Whisper/Loud

The Active Math — Whisper/Loud movements are designed to increase a child's heart rate and add additional PE minutes to the school day. All movements are intended to be performed while the child is in control of him/herself. A child who is not able to be in control is asked to sit at a desk until completion of the activity. The purpose of the whisper/loud activities is to strengthen one-to-one correspondence. There are ten movements for each multiple in this section.

Tips:

Children love to make sounds associated with the movement (ex. Vroom, vroom for the dirt bike). Allow them do so for 10 seconds or so before beginning counting.

Whenever possible, have children cross over the middle of the body (ex. left arm crossing over to the right side).

Movements for Practicing One-to-One Correspondence

Tiger Twist

Right hand to left foot "one"
Left hand to right foot "two"
Right hand to left knee "three"
Left hand to right knee "four"
Right hand to left hip "five"
Left hand to right hip "six"
Right hand to left shoulder "seven"
Left hand to right shoulder "eight"
Arms straight up sway left "nine"
Sway right "ten"
Right hand to left foot "eleven"
(continue counting pattern to 10, 20, 50 or 100...)

Active Math — Whisper/Loud

Bunny Hop

Make bunny ears with your hands by placing your hands on forehead (palms forward).
Bend left ear down (bend left-hand fingers forward) "one"
Bend right ear down (bend right-hand fingers forward) "two"
Hop "three"
(continue counting pattern to 10, 20, 50 or 100…)

Active Math — Whisper/Loud

The Counting Train

The goal is to have the children count quickly one after another forward and backward. The quicker the counting, the faster the train zooms along the tracks.

Children stand in a circle. The first student counts "one." The next student counts "two" etc. At any time, a student can say the next number then raise both hands and say "HALT." This causes the counting to go back in the other direction. For example, if the counting is "8," "9," "10," and HALT is called, the counting reverses: "9," "8," "7..."

Counting continues until all children have had a turn.

Airplane

Make airplane wings with your arms straight out at shoulder level
Lift left arm, lower right arm, glide "one"
Lift right arm, lower left arm, glide "two"
Straight arms, glide "three"
(continue counting pattern to 10, 20, 50 or 100...)

Active Math — Whisper/Loud

Climbing trees

Pretend to climb trees.
Reach left hand up and cross over right "one"
Reach right hand up and cross over left "two"
(continue counting pattern to 10, 20, 50 or 100...)

Active Math — Whisper/Loud

Tyrannosaurus Rex

Stomp left foot "one"
Stomp right foot "two"
Grab your prey "three"
(continue counting pattern to 10, 20, 50 or 100...)

Fly Fishing

With two hands, cast rod over to right "one"
With two hands, cast rod over to left "two"
(continue counting pattern to 10, 20, 50 or 100...)

Active Math — Whisper/Loud

Doggy Dig

Pretend you are dogs digging up the yard.
Dig with left hand "one"
Dig with right hand "two"
Dig with both hands "three"
(continue counting pattern to 10, 20, 50 or 100...)

Swaying Trees

It's a windy, windy day! Put your arms over your head and pretend your arms are the tree branches blowing in the wind.
Sway to the left "one"
Sway to the right "two"
Sway forwards "three"
Sway backwards "four"
(continue counting pattern to 10, 20, 50 or 100...)

Active Math — Whisper/Loud

Basketball

Dribble pretend basketball with left hand "one"
Dribble pretend basketball with right hand "two"
(continue counting pattern to 10, 20, 50 or 100...)

Active Math — Whisper/Loud

Movements for whisper/loud counting by 2's

Numbers to be whispered are in lower case. Ex. "one". Numbers to be said loudly are in capitals with an exclamation point. Ex. "TWO!"

X-Ray

Cross arms over chest "one"
Clap "TWO!"
Cross arms over chest "three"
Clap "FOUR!"
Cross arms over chest "five"
Clap "SIX!"
Cross arms over chest "seven"
Clap "EIGHT!"
Cross arms over chest "nine"
Clap "TEN!"
Cross arms over chest "eleven"
Clap "TWELVE!"
Cross arms over chest "thirteen"
Clap "FOURTEEN!"
Cross arms over chest "fifteen"
Clap "SIXTEEN!"
Cross arms over chest "seventeen"
Clap "EIGHTEEN!"
Cross arms over chest "nineteen"
Clap "TWENTY!"

Active Math — Whisper/Loud

Sky Scraper

Stand up tall.
Raise your arms up straight, point palms in and fingers pointing towards the sky (i.e. Make parallel lines with your arms. Be sure arms touch the hair on each side of your head), "one"
Clap "TWO!"
(continue on to twenty...)

Jumping for Jupiter

Bend legs in a crouched position "one"
Jump up and clap arms overhead "TWO!"
(continue on to twenty...)

Active Math — Whisper/Loud

Race Car

Hands on steering wheel, steer left "one"
Clap "TWO!"
(continue on to twenty...)

Dirt Bike

Rev your motor with your hands "one"
Clap "TWO!"
(continue on to twenty...)

Active Math — Whisper/Loud

Praying Mantis

Arms bent at elbows so hands are at shoulder-level, raise one leg with knee bent "one"
Clap, lower leg simultaneously, "TWO!"
(continue on to twenty...)

Flamingo Flaunt

Raise your leg and rest it against opposite knee, balance as you raise wings to side "one"
Clap and lower leg simultaneously, "TWO!"
(continue on to twenty, alternating legs...)

Chicken

Make chicken wings
Flap "one"
Clap "TWO!"
(continue on to twenty...)

Doggy Dig

Dig "one"
Clap "TWO!"
(continue on to twenty...)

Active Math — Whisper/Loud

Time to Clean Up

Sit on the floor, with soles of the feet together and tucked in so that your legs form wings
Bend over and pick up something from the floor "one"
Stand up straight "TWO!"
(continue on to twenty...)

Active Math — Whisper/Loud

Movements for whisper/loud counting by 3's

Numbers to be whispered are in lower case. Ex. "one". Numbers to be said loudly are in capitals with an exclamation point. Ex. "THREE!"

Cat Scratch

Pretend to be a cat and get your claws out.
Claw left "one"
Claw right "two"
Clap "THREE!"
Claw left "four"
Claw right "five"
Clap "SIX!"
Claw left "seven"
Claw right "eight"
Clap "NINE!"
Claw left "ten"
Claw right "eleven"
Clap "TWELVE!"
Claw left "thirteen"
Claw right "fourteen"
Clap "FIFTEEN!"
Claw left "sixteen"
Claw right "seventeen"
Clap "EIGHTEEN!"
Claw left "nineteen"
Claw right "twenty"
Clap "TWENTY-ONE!"
Claw left "twenty-two"
Claw right "twenty-three"
Clap "TWENTY-FOUR!"
Claw left "twenty-five"
Claw right "twenty-six"
Clap "TWENTY-SEVEN!"
Claw left "twenty-eight"
Claw right "twenty-nine"
Clap "THIRTY!"

Active Math — Whisper/Loud

Three's Dance Move

Cross right arm and leg over to the left, snap "one"
Cross left hand and leg over to the right and snap "two"
Clap "THREE!"
(continue on to thirty...)

Active Math — Whisper/Loud

Elephant March

Make your elephant trunk with the brain gym hookup (arms out straight, put right arm over left and clasp palms together, then bring arms back toward body so that clasped hands are near your chin)
Right ankle crosses over left leg "one"
Left ankle crosses over right leg "two"
Raise your trunk "THREE!"
(continue on to thirty...)

Eagle Swoop

Flap left wing "one"
Flap right wing "two"
Swoop down to catch prey. Clap "THREE!"
(continue on to thirty...)

Active Math — Whisper/Loud

Horse Gallop

Gallop to the left "one"
Gallop to the right "two"
Clap "THREE!"
(continue on to thirty...)

Sleepytime

Hands together, palms touching, like in prayer position
Go to sleep on the left "one"
Go to sleep on the right "two"
Clap "THREE!"
(continue on to thirty...)

Airplane

Arms out like wings
Swoop to the left "one"
Swoop to the right "two"
Clap "THREE!"
(continue on to thirty...)

Dirt Bike

Squeeze handle bar to the left "one"
Squeeze handle bar to the right "two"
Clap "THREE!"
(continue on to thirty...)

Active Math — Whisper/Loud

Golf Swing

Swing to the left "one"
Swing to the right "two"
Clap overhead "THREE!"
(continue on to thirty...)

Home Run

Hold your baseball bat
Swing bat to the left "one"
Swing bat to the right "two"
Jump up and clap overhead "THREE!"
(continue on to thirty...)

Active Math — Whisper/Loud

Movements for whisper/loud counting by 4's

Numbers to be whispered are in lower case. Ex. "one".
Numbers to be said loudly are in capitals with an exclamation point. Ex. "FOUR!"

Sleepy Trees

We're trees and it's a windy, windy day.
Stretch your branches up and sway to the left "one"
Sway to the right "two"
Your tree goes down to take a nap "three"
Jump up and clap "FOUR!"
Sway to the left "five"
Sway to the right "six"
Your tree goes down to take a nap "seven"
Jump up and clap "EIGHT!"
Sway to the left "nine"
Sway to the right "ten"
Your tree goes down to take a nap "eleven"
Jump up and clap "TWELVE!"
Sway to the left "thirteen"
Sway to the right "fourteen"
Your tree goes down to take a nap "fifteen"
Jump up and clap "SIXTEEN!"
Sway to the left "seventeen"
Sway to the right "eighteen"
Your tree goes down to take a nap "nineteen"
Jump up and clap "TWENTY!"
Sway to the left "twenty-one"
Sway to the right "twenty-two"
Your tree goes down to take a nap "twenty-three"
Jump up and clap "TWENTY-FOUR!"
Sway to the left "twenty-five"
Sway to the right "twenty-six"
Your tree goes down to take a nap "twenty-seven"
Jump up and clap "TWENTY-EIGHT!"
(continue to forty...)

Active Math — Whisper/Loud

Criss Cross for 4's

This exercise is similar to doing "windmills."
Spread legs, bend over.
Touch right hand to left foot "one"
Touch left hand to right foot "two"
Cross hands over chest, so that right hand is on left shoulder, left hand on right shoulder "three"
Clap "FOUR!"
(continue on to forty...)

4's Twist

Touch right hand to bottom of left foot "one"
Touch left hand to bottom of right foot "two"
Cross hands over chest, so that right hand is on left shoulder, left hand on right shoulder "three"
Clap "FOUR!"
(continue on to forty...)

The Fours Stretch

Stand up straight with arms at sides.
Lean over and touch toes "one"
Touch knees "two"
Put hands on hips "three"
Clap "FOUR!"
(continue on to forty...)

Puffin Moves

Waddle to the left "one"
Waddle to the right "two"
Paddle in the ocean "three"
Clap "FOUR!"
(continue on to forty...)

37

Active Math — Whisper/Loud

Doggy Dig

Both paws dig to the left "one"
Dig to the right "two"
Dig in the middle "three"
Clap "FOUR!"
(continue on to forty...)

Basketball

Dribble to the left "one"
Dribble to the right "two"
Shoot up high with both hands "three"
Clap "FOUR!"
(continue on to forty...)

Fishing

Get your rod and cast to the left "one"
Cast to the right "two"
Reel in that fish "three"
Clap "FOUR!"
(continue on to forty...)

Helicopter Twirl

Lift your arms straight up overhead with palms together.
Twirl arms on the left side "one"
Twirl arms on the right side "two"
Twirl in the middle with big circles "three"
Clap "FOUR!"
(continue on to forty...)

Paddle the Canoe

Pretend you are in a canoe.
Paddle to the left "one"
Paddle to the right "two"
Balance yourself "three"
Clap "FOUR!"
(continue on to forty...)

Active Math — Whisper/Loud

Movements for whisper/loud counting by 5's

Numbers to be whispered are in lower case. Ex. "one". Numbers to be said loudly are in capitals with an exclamation point. Ex. "FIVE!"

5's Twist

Touch right hand to bottom of left foot "one"
Touch left and to bottom of right foot "two"
Touch right elbow to left knee "three"
Touch left elbow to right knee "four"
Clap "FIVE!"
(continue on to fifty...)

Criss Cross for 5's

Spread legs, bend over.
Touch right hand to left foot "one"
Touch left hand to right foot "two"
Touch right hand to left knee "three"
Touch left hand to right knee "four"
Clap "FIVE!"
(continue on to fifty...)

Clever Kitten

Get out your kitten claws!
Scratch with your left hand "one"
Scratch with your right hand "two"
Put your hands on your hips.
Wag your kitten tail to the left "three"
Wag your kitten tail to the right "four"
Clap "FIVE!"
(continue on to fifty...)

Active Math — Whisper/Loud

Tyrannosaurus Rex

Reach out and grab your prey with your left hand "one"
Reach out and grab your prey with your right hand "two"
Eat your prey with your left hand "three"
Eat your prey with your right hand "four"
Clap "FIVE!"
(continue on to fifty...)

Pterodactyl

Make Pterodactyl wings with your outstretched arms.
Raise left arm and lower right "one"
Raise right arm and lower left "two"
With both hands, pounce down to ground to left "three"
With both hands, pounce down to ground to right "four"
Clap "FIVE!"
(continue on to fifty...)

Brontosaurus

Make the Brontosaurus's long neck with your two outstretched arms.
Reach down with your long neck and nibble a plant to the left "one"
Reach down with your long neck and nibble a plant to the right "two"
Reach up with your long neck and nibble a plant to the left "three"
Reach up with your long neck and nibble a plant to the right "four"
Clap "FIVE!"
(continue on to fifty...)

Active Math — Whisper/Loud

Tie Your Shoes

Bend over left foot and tie shoe with left hand "one" then with right hand "two"
Bend over right foot and tie shoe with left hand "three" then with right hand "four"
Clap "FIVE!"
(continue on to fifty...)

Set the Table

Lay out the napkin with left hand "one"
Lay out the fork with left hand "two"
Lay out the knife with right hand "three"
Lay out the spoon with right hand "four"
Clap "FIVE!"
(continue on to fifty...)

Drummers

Make drumsticks with your two hands.
Beat the drum with both hands to left and up "one"
Beat the drum with both hands to right and up "two"
Beat the drum with both hands to left and down "three"
Beat the drum with both hands to right and down "four"
Clap "FIVE!"
(continue on to fifty...)

Ride Your Bike

Climb on bike "one"
Balance bike with outstretched arms "two"
Pedal bike "three"
Balance bike with outstretched arms "four"
Clap "FIVE!"
(continue on to fifty...)

Active Math — Whisper/Loud

Movements for whisper/loud counting by 6's

Numbers to be whispered are in lower case. Ex. "one". Numbers to be said loudly are in capitals with an exclamation point. Ex. "SIX!"

Criss Cross for 6

Spread legs, bend over.
Touch right hand to left foot "one"
Touch left hand to right foot "two"
Touch right hand to left knee "three"
Touch left hand to right knee "four"
Cross arms over chest, so that your right hand is on your left shoulder, left hand on right shoulder "five"
Clap "SIX!"
Touch right hand to left foot "seven"
Touch left hand to right foot "eight"
Touch right hand to left knee "nine"
Touch left hand to right knee "ten"
Cross arms over chest "eleven"
Clap "TWELVE!"

(continue on to sixty…)

Active Math — Whisper/Loud

6's Twist

Touch right hand to bottom of left foot "one"
Touch left hand to bottom of right foot "two"
Touch right elbow to left knee "three"
Touch left elbow to right knee "four"
Cross hands over chest, so that right hand is on left shoulder, left hand on right shoulder "five"
Clap "SIX!"
(continue on to sixty...)

Jaguar Tummy Rub

Put your hands on your hips.
Cross right ankle over left leg "one"
Cross left ankle over right leg "two"
Wag your tail to the left "three"
Wag your tail to the right "four"
Rub the tummy "five
Clap "SIX!"
(continue on to sixty...)

Bear Scratch

Get down on all fours.
Lift left paw "one"
Lift right paw "two"
Lift back left paw "three"
Lift back right paw "four"
Scratch "five"
Clap "SIX!"
(continue on to sixty...)

Active Math — Whisper/Loud

Chimpanzee Flick

Climb left "one", climb right "two"
Twist left "three", twist right "four"
Flick the flea "five"
Clap "SIX!"
(continue on to sixty...)

Donkey Kick

Get down on all fours.
Stomp left front hoof "one"
Stomp right front hoof "two"
Stomp back left hoof "three"
Stomp back right hoof "four"
Kick both front legs up "five"
Clap "SIX!"
(continue on to sixty...)

Apple Picking

Left hand crosses over up high to pick an apple "one"
Right hand crosses over up high to pick an apple "two"
Left hand crosses over at chest level "three"
Right hand crosses over at chest level "four"
Take a bite "five"
Clap "SIX!"
(continue on to sixty...)

Making Lemonade

Left hand crosses over to pick a lemon "one"
Right hand crosses over to pick a lemon "two"
Cross over to squeeze it left "three"
Cross over to squeeze it right "four"
Take a drink "five"
Clap "SIX!"
(continue on to sixty...)

Active Math — Whisper/Loud

Clean the house

Right hand vacuums to the left "one"
Left hand vacuums to the right "two"
Right hand dusts up high left "three"
Left hand dusts up high right "four"
Wipe brow with back of hand "five"
Clap "SIX!"
(continue on to sixty…)

Volleyball

Bump the ball to the left "one"
Bump the ball to the right "two"
Set to the left "three"
Set to the right "four"
Spike "five"
Clap "SIX!"
(continue on to sixty…)

Football

Pass the ball to the left "one"
Pass the ball to the right "two"
Catch the ball on the left "three"
Catch the ball on the right "four"
Run for a touchdown "five"
Clap "SIX!"
(continue on to sixty…)

Active Math — Whisper/Loud

Movements for whisper/loud counting by 7's

Numbers to be whispered are in lower case. Ex. "one". Numbers to be said loudly are in capitals with an exclamation point. Ex. "SEVEN!"

7's Twist

Right hand to bottom of left foot "one"
Left hand to bottom of right foot "two"
Right elbow to left knee "three"
Left elbow to right knee "four"
Twist to the left "five"
Twist to the right "six"
Clap "SEVEN!"
(continue on to seventy...)

Active Math — Whisper/Loud

Criss Cross for 7's

Spread legs, bend over.
Right hand to left foot "one"
Left hand to right foot "two"
Right hand to left knee "three"
Left hand to right knee "four"
Right hand to left hip "five"
Left hand to right hip "six"
Clap "SEVEN!"
(continue on to seventy...)

Gorilla Games

Climb a tree to the left "one"
Climb a tree to the right "two"
Beat your chest (right fist to left shoulder) "three"
Beat your chest (left fist to right shoulder) "four"
Pick a banana "five"
Pick a banana "six"
Clap "SEVEN!"
(continue on to seventy...)

Kangaroo Konga

Hop forward "one"
Hop backward "two"
Hop to the left "three"
Hop to the right "four"
Pat your joey with your left hand "five"
Pat your joey with your right hand "six"
Clap "SEVEN!"
(continue on to seventy...)

Active Math — Whisper/Loud

Lion Lick

Down on all fours:
Lift front left leg "one"
Lift front right leg "two"
Lift back left leg "three"
Life back right leg "four"
Pretend to lick your left front leg "five"
Pretend to lick your right front leg "six"
Clap "SEVEN!"
(continue on to seventy...)

Fly Fishing

Clasp hands around your fishing rod up high
Cast to the left "one"
Cast to the right "two"
Cast sideways to the left "three"
Cast sideways to the right "four"
Cast from down low coming up left "five"
Cast from down low coming up right "six"
Clap "SEVEN!"
(continue on to seventy...)

Pillow Fight

Hold onto your pillow up high
Hit above to the left "one"
Hit above to the right "two"
Hit waist level left "three"
Hit waist level right "four"
Hit down low left "five"
Hit down low right "six"
Clap "SEVEN!"
(continue on to seventy...)

Active Math — Whisper/Loud

Book Report

Choose a book to the left "one"
Choose a book to the right "two"
Read a book in your left hand "three"
Read a book a book in your right hand "four"
Write the report with your left hand "five"
Write the report with your right hand "six"
Clap "SEVEN!"
(continue on to seventy...)

Hockey

Hit the puck to the left "one"
Hit the puck to the right 'two"
Skate the left foot across to the right "three"
Skate the right foot "four"
High five to the left "five"
High five to the right "six"
Clap "SEVEN!"
(continue on to seventy...)

Swimming

Front stroke with left arm "one"
Front Stroke with right arm "two"
Back Stroke with left arm "three"
Back Stroke with right arm "four"
Side Stroke with left arm "five"
Side Stroke with right arm "six"
Clap "SEVEN!"
(continue on to seventy...)

Active Math — Whisper/Loud

8's Twist

Right hand to bottom of left foot "one"
Left hand to bottom of right foot "two"
Right elbow to left knee "three"
Left elbow to right knee "four"
Twist to the left "five"
Twist to the right "six"
Cross arms over chest "seven"
Clap "EIGHT!"
(continue on to eighty...)

Movements for whisper/loud counting by 8's

Numbers to be whispered are in lower case. Ex. "one". Numbers to be said loudly are in capitals. Ex. "EIGHT!"

Active Math — Whisper/Loud

Criss Cross for 8's

Spread legs, bend over.
Right hand to left foot "one"
Left hand to right foot "two"
Right hand to left knee "three"
Left hand to right knee "four"
Right hand to left hip "five"
Left hand to right hip "six"
Cross arms over chest "seven"
Clap "EIGHT!"
 (continue on to eighty...)

Giraffe in the Jungle

Legs apart, Arms stretched up overhead, fingers clasped together, to make a long neck
Cross Right ankle over left "one"
Cross left ankle over right "two"
Reach left to get a leaf "three"
Reach right to get a leaf "four"
Reach down left to get a leaf "five"
Reach down right to get a leaf "six"
Bend down to get a drink "seven"
Clap "EIGHT!"
 (continue on to eighty...)

Tiger Tail Twirl

Hold tail in your hand and twirl it around
Jump over tail to the left "one"
Jump over tail to the right "two"
Swing tail to the left "three"
Swing tail to the right "four"
Wag the tail to the left "five"
Wag the tail to the right "six"
Stroke the tail "seven"
Clap "EIGHT!"
 (continue on to eighty...)

Active Math — Whisper/Loud

Flashing Fish

Put hands, palms together in prayer position, out front
Swim down to the left "one"
Swim down to the right "two"
Swim to the side left "three"
Swim to the side right "four"
Swim up left "five"
Swim up right "six"
Jump straight up out of water "seven"
Clap "EIGHT!"
(continue on to eighty...)

Cherry Pie

Cross over reach up high to pick cherries left "one"
Cross over reach up high to pick cherries right "two"
Cross over to pit cherries to the left "three"
Cross over to pit cherries to the right "four"
Pat the dough left "five"
Pat the dough right "six"
Take a bite "seven"
Clap "EIGHT!"
(continue on to eighty...)

Clean Car

Pick up trash left "one"
Pick up trash right "two"
Wash windows left "three"
Wash windows right "four"
Vacuum the car left "five"
Vacuum the car right "six"
Wipe your brow "seven"
Clap "EIGHT!"
(continue on to eighty...)

Active Math — Whisper/Loud

Tennis

Forehand stroke to the left "one"
Back hand stroke to the left "two"
Volley stroke left "three"
Volley stroke right "four"
First serve left "five"
Second serve right "six"
Ready position "seven"
Clap "EIGHT!"
(continue on to eighty...)

Football for Eights

Throw the ball to the left "one"
Throw the ball to the right "two"
Block to the left "three"
Block to the right "four"
Catch the ball left "five"
Catch the ball right "six"
Run in for the touchdown "seven"
Clap "EIGHT!"
(continue on to eighty...)

Baseball

Throw the ball to the left "one"
Throw the ball to the right "two"
Hit the ball to the left "three"
Hit the ball to the right "four"
Catch the ball on the left "five"
Catch the ball on the right "six"
Run to base "seven"
Clap "EIGHT!"
(continue on to eighty...)

Active Math — Whisper/Loud

Movements for whisper/loud counting by 9's

Numbers to be whispered are in lower case. Ex. "one". Numbers to be said loudly are in capitals. Ex. "NINE!"

9's Twist

Right hand to bottom of left foot "one"
Left hand to bottom of right foot "two"
Right elbow to left knee "three"
Left elbow to right knee "four"
Twist to the left "five"
Twist to the right "six"
Reach up, sway left "seven"
Reach up, sway right "eight"
Clap up high "NINE!"
(continue on to ninety...)

Active Math — Whisper/Loud

Criss Cross for 9's

Spread legs, bend over.
Right hand to left foot "one"
Left hand to right foot "two"
Right hand to left knee "three"
Left hand to right knee "four"
Right hand to left hip "five"
Left hand to right hip "six"
Right hand to left shoulder "seven"
Left hand to right shoulder "eight"
Clap "NINE!" (continue on to ninety...)

Tarantula Tantrum for 9's

Cross left leg over right and shake it "one"
Cross right leg over left and shake it "two"
Stomp left foot "three"
Stomp right foot "four"
Make fist with hand. Cross left hand over right and shake fist "five"
Make fist with hand. Cross right hand over left and shake fist "six"
Raise left fist in the air and shake it "seven"
Raise right fist in the air and shake it "eight"
Clap "NINE!" (continue on to ninety...)

Polar Bear Brunch

Grab a fish with your left hand "one"
Grab a fish with right hand "two"
Eat a fish with your left hand "three"
Eat a fish with your right hand "four"
Play with your cubs, Twist to the left "five"
Play with your cubs, Twist to the right "six"
Take a nap on the left "seven"
Take a nap on the right "eight"
Clap "NINE!" (continue on to ninety...)

Active Math — Whisper/Loud

Zebra Zeal

Gallop forward "one"
Gallop backward "two"
Gallop to the left "three"
Gallop to the right "four"
Rear up "five"
Rear up "six"
Reach for grass "seven"
Eat grass "eight"
Clap "NINE!"
(continue on to ninety...)

Panda Push-ups

Down on all fours
Push up left "one"
Push up right "two"
Lift left leg up "three"
Lift right leg up "four"
Chin up (wrap both hands around a pretend bar) to the left "five"
Chin up to the right "six"
Climb a tree "seven"
Climb a tree "eight"
Clap "NINE!" (continue on to ninety...)

Food Fight

Throw a banana to the left "one"
Throw a banana to the right "two"
Watch out! Twist to the left "three"
Twist to the right "four"
Throw some noodles to the left "five"
Throw some noodles to the right "six"
Pick food out of your hair left "seven"
Pick food out of your hair right "eight"
Clap "NINE!"
(continue on to ninety...)

Active Math — Whisper/Loud

Berry Picking

Pick berries near your toes to the left "one"
Pick berries near your toes to the right "two"
Pick berries near your knees to the left "three"
Pick berries near your knees to the right "four"
Pick berries near your hips to the left "five"
Pick berries near your hips to the right "six"
Pick berries up high to the left "seven"
Pick berries up high to the right "eight"
Clap "NINE!"
(continue on to ninety...)

Basket ball Bump

Dribble to the left "one"
Dribble to the right "two"
Pass to the left "three"
Pass to the right "four"
Catch to the right "five"
Catch to the right "six"
Shoot to the left "seven"
Shoot to the right "eight"
Clap "NINE!"
(continue on to ninety...)

Soccer Stars

Run to the left "one"
Run to the right "two"
Kick the ball to the left "three"
Kick the ball to the right "four"
Stop the ball on the left "five"
Stop the ball on the right "six"
Head the ball to the left "seven"
Head the ball to the right "eight"
Clap "NINE!"
(continue on to ninety...)

Active Math — Skip Counting

The Active Math—Skip Counting Movements are designed to provide fun, physical drills for basic math skills learning. The more times a child skip counts, the faster the skip counting patterns become established in a child's brain. Children enjoy the process of learning to skip count when it is combined with gross motor physical activity. Learning to skip count can be considered the ABC's of math. Learning to read is facilitated when children know the alphabet. When children know how to skip count, they can utilize this knowledge to facilitate learning multiplication, division, factoring, algebra and other more advanced math.

The activities in this section can be used in the classroom, during recess, physical education class or while waiting for the commencement of art, music or lunch. There are 104 suggested activities. They are sorted by letters of the alphabet so that they can be included with letter of the week activities. Strive to do a minimum of three activities each day and encourage your students to think of other activities that start with the letter of the week.

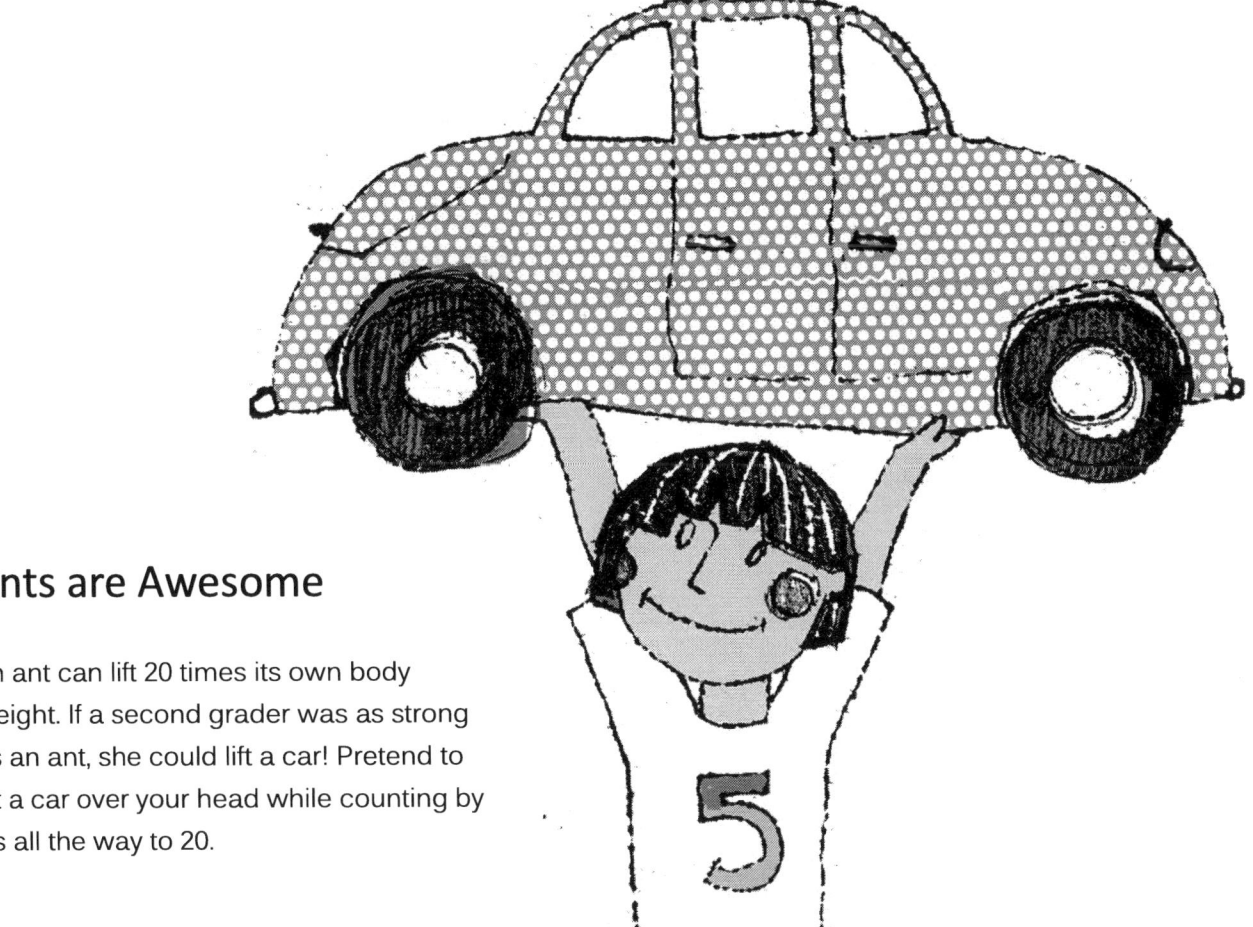

Ants are Awesome

An ant can lift 20 times its own body weight. If a second grader was as strong as an ant, she could lift a car! Pretend to lift a car over your head while counting by 2's all the way to 20.

Active Math — Skip Counting

Antelope Antics

One species of antelope, the klipspringer, has tiny, rounded hooves with a pad in the center that acts like a suction cup, so these nimble antelope can hop from rock to rock without falling. Hop from rock to rock while skip counting by any number.

April

April is the 4th month of the year. Hop on one foot as you skip count by 4's all the way to 40.

August

August is the 8th month of the year. Grab your pretend lawn mower and mow the lawn as you skip count by 8's all the way to 80.

Buzzing Bees

A honey bee can fly up to 12 miles per hour. Its wings beat 200 times per second. Beat your honey bee wings and skip count by any number.

Baseball Basics

Though it is called a baseball diamond, the infield where baseball is played is actually a square measuring 90 ft from base to base. If you don't believe us, take a look next time you're on the field. For now, batter up! Get your bat and swing at the ball while you skip count by 9's all the way to 90.

Active Math — Skip Counting

Basketball Drill

Grab your pretend ball and dribble. Dribble with your left hand, dribble with your right, just keep that ball moving. And don't forget to skip count! If real basketballs are available and space permits— use the real thing!

Beautiful Ballerinas

Both male and female ballet dancers glide gracefully across the stage. Glide across the room while you skip count by any number. Watch out for the other dancers.

Crazy Cars

Get behind the wheel of your crazy car, steering left and then right while you skip count by any number.

Crocodiles

Crocodiles use their long oar-like tails to propel themselves through the water. Clasp your hands behind your back to make a tail and swim like a crocodile as you skip count by any number.

Crunch and Count

Get down on the floor, knees bent with hands behind your head. It's crunch time! Do your crunches while skip counting by any number. (Be sure to keep the small of your back pressed against the floor.)

Active Math — Skip Counting

Cheerleaders

Get your pom-poms. Jump, shake them, and punch them in the air as you skip count by any number.

Daring Downhill

Get your skis and swoosh down the slopes while you skip count by any number.

Delicious Donuts

Can you eat 90 donuts? Devour those donuts while skip counting by 9, all the way to 90.

Disco Dancing

Pretend you're wearing a shiny shirt under flashing lights, and put on your best disco moves while you skip count by any number. (Don't know how to disco? Just dance! In this case, the sillier your moves are, the better.)

Detect that Metal

Get your metal detector and see what you can find. Skip count by 4's and when you hit 40, pretend you found something interesting.

Active Math — Skip Counting

Dig for Treasure

Whether by map, or with a metal detector, you are sure there is treasure below. Get your shovel and dig as you skip count by any number.

Drummer's Delight

Whether it's a base drum, a snare, or a full set, get your sticks and play your drum as you skip count by any number.

Elephant Ears

Place your palms on the side of your head above your ears. Now you have elephant ears. When they are hot, elephants flap their ears to circulate and cool their blood. Flap your elephant ears and skip count by any number.

Energetic Eels

Eels are legendary climbers. Young eels will climb waterfalls by leaving the water and wriggling over damp areas. This way, it is possible for them to climb a waterfall of up to 65 feet. Put your arms flat against your sides and wriggle your way up a waterfall as you skip count by any number.

Eagles' Eyesight

The bald eagle is the United States national bird. Did you know that an eagle has excellent eyesight and can lift 4 pounds? Eagles can fly up to 10,000 feet, and their wingspan can be 90 inches. Pretend you are an eagle flapping your wings and soar through the mountains. Flap your wings while you skip count by any number!

Active Math — Skip Counting

Elastic Energy Exercises

Time to energize yourself with stretching exercises! Pretend your body is an elastic rubber band. Stretch your body up, reaching toward the ceiling and then down to your toes while skip counting by any number.

February

February is the 2nd month of the year. Grab your poles and skis and pretend you are swishing down the slopes as you skip count by 2's all the way to 20.

Flying is Fantastic

Airplanes use propellers or jet engines. Birds use strong muscles in their breasts to flap their wings. What will you use? Extend your wings and soar through the sky while skip counting by 8's all the way to 80.

Figure Skating

Put space between yourself and your classmates. Hold on to your desk or the wall. Pretend you are a figure skater and twirl while skip counting by any number.

Funny Faces

Make the funniest face possible. Make funny faces while you skip count by any number.

Active Math — Skip Counting

Gorgeous Giant

The General Grant Sequoia tree in California is somewhere between 1,500 to 2,000 years old and stands at over 267 feet tall. Imagine you are this gorgeous giant and a stretch yourself up tall, with your limbs reaching toward the sky. Sway in the wind as you skip count by any number.

Gertrude the Great

In 1926, Gertrude Ederle was the first woman ever to swim the English Channel from France to England. She was 19 years and set a new world record. Are you ready to swim? Choose your stroke and brave the icy waters as you skip count by any number.

Gourmet Chef

Don your big white chef's hat and whip up something special. Chop, sauté, mix... whatever you want, while you skip count by any number.

Giraffe Giant Tongue

Giraffes have a 21 inch tongue that helps them pluck leaves from branches. Reach your arms above your head, clasp your hands together, and pretend your arms are a giraffe's long neck. Stretch out and pretend to nibble leaves from the branches as you skip count by any number.

Hammer Time

No doubt about it, a hammer is a useful tool. But did you know that for any hammering job, you should wear safety goggles? Get those goggles on and hammer away as you skip count by any number.

Active Math — Skip Counting

Happy Hugs

Spread your arms wide then give yourself a great big hug. Do it again, and keep it going as you skip count by any number.

Hay is for Horses

Hop on your imaginary horse and allow your hungry horse to gallop to the barn while skip counting by any number.

Home Run

Congratulations, you have just hit a home run! The crowd is going wild with excitement! Grab your baseball cap and run around the bases as you skip count by any number.

Ice Cream Extravaganza

You are about the make the biggest pretend ice cream sundae in the world! Scoop lots of ice cream and cover it in toppings while you skip count by any number.

Innocent Iguanas

Iguanas lay as many as 50 eggs at a time, in holes in the ground called burrows. They also dig pretend burrows to confuse any animals that may be looking for eggs to eat. Once they lay the eggs, they leave them and do not return. When iguana babies hatch, they are on their own. Pretend you are a mama iguana digging a burrow while you skip count by any number.

Active Math — Skip Counting

Interesting Insects

It is estimated that there are approximately 10 quintillion (10,000,000,000,000,000,000) individual insects alive at this time. Insects are small and, most of them fly to keep themselves safe! Flap your tiny insect wings and fly away while skip counting by any number.

Intelligent Inventors

Inventors have invented telephones, cars, computers, bikes, video games and microwaves. Hold the phone to your ear and make a call as you skip count by any number.

Jumping Jack Jaguars

Pretend to be jaguars in your African jungle school. It is time for PE class and jumping jacks. Do jumping jacks and count 4, 8, 12... 40 or 9, 18, 27...90.

Jolly Jump Ropers

It is time to jump rope. Grab your pretend jump rope and start hopping while skip counting by any number. If real jump ropes are available and space permits—use the real thing!

Jogging in the Jungle

Pretend you are in the jungle. Jog in place while skip counting by any number. Watch out for vines and branches!

Active Math — Skip Counting

Juggling on Jupiter

Pretend you are on the planet Jupiter. Pretend to juggle while skip counting by any number.

July

July is the 7th month of the year. Pretend you are swimming, using your favorite stroke as you skip count by 7's all the way to 70.

June

June is the 6th month of the year. Pretend to throw a ball as you skip count by 6's all the way to 60. If you have the real thing, and space permits, get a partner and toss the ball back and forth while you count.

Kangaroo Rats

Kangaroo rats are small animals with large back legs that enable them to jump up to 9 feet in the air in order to escape predators. Jump as far as you can while skip counting by 9's. If space doesn't allow, then jump up and down in place.

Kettledrums

Did you know that each kettledrum can be tuned to a different pitch? Tune your drums, grab your pretend sticks and beat out a rhythm while you skip count by any number.

Active Math — Skip Counting

Ketchup

Ketchup is tasty, but wouldn't it be fun to paint with, too? Imagine a squeezy bottle of ketchup in each of your hands and a huge canvas in front of you. Squeeze out a design while you skip count by any number. (Remember, this is just for pretend, and not something to try at home!)

Kites to New Heights

Whether yours is a diamond, a bat or a box kite, reel out that kite string and let it soar while you skip count by any number.

(Camouflaged) Koalas

Look way up in that Eucalyptus Tree. Is that dappled sunlight you see or a koala? The spots on their backs make it difficult to tell. Climb up to the top of that tree to see for yourself, while skip counting by any number.

Lions are Never Lonely

Lion cubs are raised by a pride of lions that usually includes five to ten female lions, and two to three males. Be a lion in your pride, get down on all fours if you want, and skip count by any number.

Lazy Lambs

We don't want our lambs to be lazy! Did you know that people who raise lambs often take them for walks? Let's slip a halter on our lambs and take them for a long walk while we skip count by any number.

Active Math — Skip Counting

Little Lady Bugs

Did you know that lady bugs are carnivores? Their favorite food is an aphid. Some Lady bugs are red with black spots, though others have no spots. Lady bugs beat their wings 85 times a second when they fly. Beat your lady bug wings and skip count by any number.

Lightweight Champion

Hooray! You are the world's lightweight boxing champion! Make fists with your hands and put your arms up in the air as you skip count by any number.

Magical Moustache

Smooth your pretend moustache while skip counting by any number.

Monkeys in the Mountains

Did you know that in the mountains of Nagano, Japan there is a place called Monkey Park? There, snow monkeys play, sun, swim and sleep while tourists take their pictures! Get out your camera and take pictures, or pretend to be a playful monkey, while you skip count by any number.

Magnificent Moose

Did you know that moose are the largest members of the deer family? Male moose grow huge antlers on their heads each year that can weigh up to 75 lbs. They can run as fast as 35 miles per hour, and are good swimmers. Get down on all fours and pretend you're a moose as you skip count by any number.

Active Math — Skip Counting

March

March is the 3rd month of the year. March in place as you skip count by 3's all the way to 30.

May

May is the 5th month of the year. If space permits, skip around the room while you skip count by 5's all the way to 50. If space doesn't allow, then hop in place.

Nice Narwhale

The male narwhale has a long spiral tusk extending from his upper jaw. Raise and clasp hands straight over your head to make a long tusk extending from your forehead. Skip count by any number.

Nervous Nelly

What happens to you when you're nervous? Do you shake all over? Pretend you are nervous now as you skip count by any number.

Nurse Sharks

Nurse sharks are slow-moving bottom dwellers that use their strong jaws to crush and eat shellfish and even coral, but prefer to dine on fish, shrimp, and squid. Pretend you're a nurse shark, skimming the bottom of the ocean, as you skip count by any number.

Active Math — Skip Counting

Nuts and Bolts

Have you ever thought about what our world would be like without nuts and bolts? They, and other fasteners, hold so many things together. A car, for example, has about 3,500 fasteners. Grab your screwdriver, some nuts and some bolts. What will you fasten together, while skip counting by any number?

Never a Numbat in the Netherlands

Numbats are diurnal marsupials that live in Australia and exist mostly on termites. Pretend to dig for termites while skip counting by any number.

Outrageous Owls

Most owls are nocturnal hunters, meaning they hunt for prey at night. One method they use is called "perch and pounce." Imagine you are an owl perched on a tree branch, then swoop down to catch your prey as you skip count by 2's all the way to 20. (i.e. Perch "two," swoop "four," perch "six," swoop "eight" and so on....)

Orcas

Orcas, or killer whales, are the largest of the dolphins. They can weigh up to six tons and have teeth that can be four inches long. Imagine you are an orca, swimming with your pod in cold, ocean waters while you skip count by any number.

Active Math — Skip Counting

One Octopus

An octopus is probably one of the cleverest animals in the ocean. A speedy swimmer and crafty hunter, the octopus uses its eight tentacles to full advantage. Pretend you have eight long tentacles as you move through the ocean and skip count by 8's all the way to 80.

October

October is the 10th month of the year. Do jumping jacks while you skip count by 10 all the way to 100.

Painting Party

Gather your friends and paint the back fence. Imagine whatever colors you like as you take broad strokes to get the job done. And don't forget to skip count!

Panda Push-ups

Can you do push-ups better than a panda? Get down on the floor and do push-ups while you skip count by 2's all the way to 20.

Penguin Parade

Glue your arms to your sides and walk like a penguin while you skip count by any number.

Active Math — Skip Counting

Ponytail

Comb your hair and fasten it into a ponytail while you skip count by any number. (Those with short hair can just comb hair.)

Quaking, Queasy Queen

Pretend you are a queen on a ship in the middle of the ocean. The ship is rocking you while you skip count by any number.

Quarterback Facts

The quarterback touches the ball on nearly every offensive play and has a great deal of responsibility both in calling plays and making decisions during the play. Most quarterbacks are on the field for every offensive play leaving only for injury or when the game's outcome is no longer in doubt. Pretend you're the quarterback of your favorite team. Receive the ball from the huddle, run, pass and catch as you skip count by any number.

Quiet Quilting

You've already pieced together and sewn a beautiful pattern with scraps of colorful fabric; now all you have to do is quilt it! In free motion quilting, you use both hands to guide the fabric up, down, side-to-side and all around as it moves through the sewing machine. Use your hands to make an amazing pattern, and don't forget to push the foot pedal to keep the machine going as you skip count by any number.

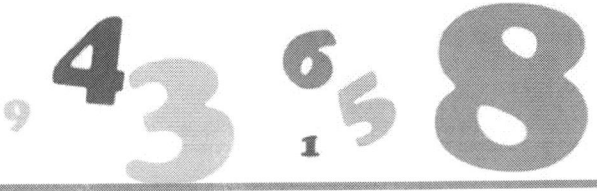

Active Math — Skip Counting

Quetzals Are Colorful

The resplendent quetzal lives in the mountainous cloud forests in Central America. These quetzals are about 14 inches long, but the male's colorful tail can extend as much as thirty inches. He has a red breast and his other feathers are blue, green, yellow, and white. Though they are beautiful, they are poor flyers. Pretend you are a quetzal and preen your feathers while you skip count by any number.

Quail Coveys

Many quail chicks are quite mature and mobile from the moment of hatching, so they can leave the nest with their parents. They are ground-dwelling birds, but will burst into short, fast flight if disturbed. Put your hands on your hips and do a quail walk as you skip count by any number.

Rabbit

The world record for the rabbit long jump is 3 meters. That's over 9 feet! You don't have to do the long jump to pretend to be a rabbit. How about hopping in place while you count by 9's all the way to 90?

Rapid Reindeer

A day-old reindeer calf can outrun a full-grown man. How fast can you run? If space allows, run around while skip counting by any number, otherwise, jog in place.

Reaching for the Sky

Stand with your legs apart and reach up as far as you can, first with your left arm and then with your right while skip counting by any number.

Active Math — Skip Counting

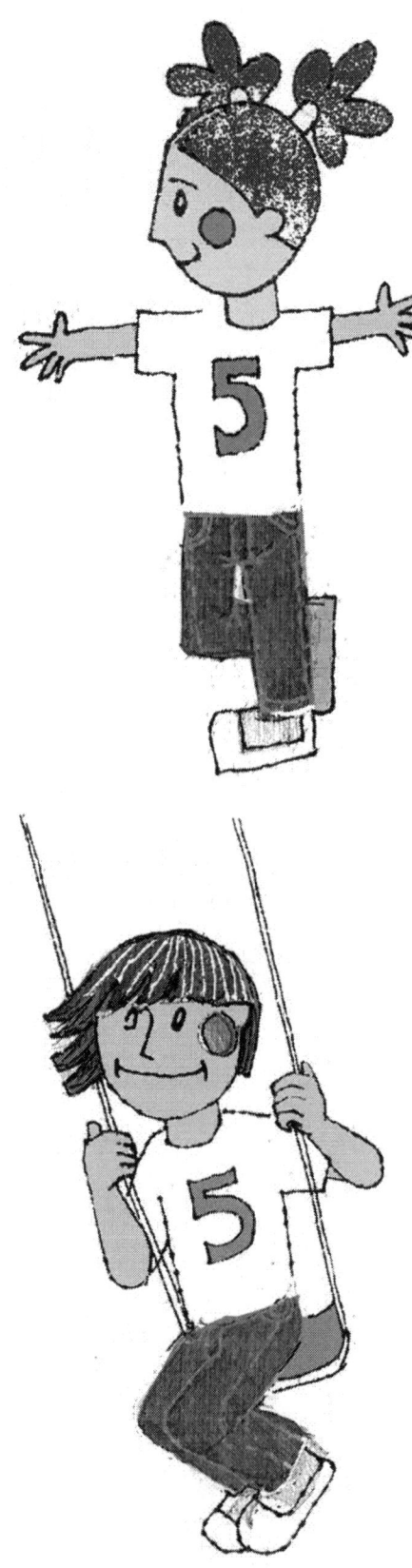

Romping Rhinos

Rhinos weigh over two tons and have poor eyesight. Paw the ground with one foot as you skip count by any number.

September

September is the 9th month of the year. Grab your pretend eraser and erase your classroom chalk board or white board as you skip count by nine all the way to 90's. If that board is really messy, you might need to use two hands!

Skip Counting on the Swings

Time to go outside and use the swings! As you swing forward, count 3; backward, count 6; forward again, count 9 etc. or skip count by any other number.

Seals Scolding

Mommy seals are scolding their babies for swimming too close to polar bears. Hold out one finger and pretend to scold your baby seal while skip counting by any number.

Slow Snails

Clasp hands together and pretend to be a snail slowly slithering along while skip counting by any number.

Active Math — Skip Counting

Terrific Toads

Toads are known for being able to jump quickly. Can you? Get down in toad position and see how far you can jump while skip counting by any number. (If space is tight, hop in place.)

Temper Tantrum

Beat your fists on your desk or your lap and make a mad face while you skip count by any number.

Touch Those Toes

Stand with your feet hip-width apart, then bending at the waist, touch your right foot with your left hand, then your left foot with your right hand while skip counting by any number.

Tiger Tails

Did you know that every tiger has a unique pattern of stripes? Tigers can weigh 720 pounds and can have a three foot long tail. Twirl your tail as you skip count by any number.

Ultimate Frisbee

Grab your disc. Throw and catch while you skip count by any number. (If real Frisbees are available and space permits—pair up and use the real thing!)

Active Math — Skip Counting

Unwrap the Ukulele

Did you know the name "ukulele" actually means "jumping flea" in Hawaiian? Could it be because a player's fingers jump up and down the stringed board quickly? Whatever the reason, unwrap your ukulele and play a tune while you skip count by any number.

Ultra Umbrella

There is a hurricane and you need your ultra umbrella to protect you from the rain. Skip count by any number as you open the umbrella.

Use the Umiak when it's Urgent

You are an Eskimo living in Alaska. You have just received an urgent message that you have to deliver. Paddle your umiak to deliver your message while skip counting by any number.

Voyage on the Vast Sea

Choose your vessel and climb aboard. Watch out for those waves as you skip count by any number.

Vacuum

Plug in your vacuum cleaner and go to work, as you skip count by any number.

Active Math — Skip Counting

Very Video

Get out your video camera and take some footage while skip counting by any number.

Violin

Resin up that bow and play a tune on your violin while you skip count by any number.

Volleyball

Whether you're setting, digging, spiking, blocking or serving, volleyball is fun! So play some volleyball while skip counting by any number.

Vicuna

A Vicuna is a cud chewing animal of the camel family living in the South American Andes. At 90 pounds, it is the smallest of all camels. Pretend to chew your cud while you skip count by 9's all the way to 90.

Wash the Car Windows

It's been a dirty, dusty summer. Don't forget to squeegee the windows dry as you skip count by any number.

Wild Weather

It's snowing, it's blowing and you're outside! Skip count by any number as you move about and try to stay warm.

Active Math — Skip Counting

Wiggle Worm

Glue your arms to your sides and wiggle like a worm while you skip count by any number.

Windmill

It's a windy day and you are a windmill. Crank those arms and skip count by any number.

X's are Excellent

Stand with your feet together and your arms by your side. Now jump your feet out to more than hip-width apart, and bring your arms up so your body makes an X. (like a jumping jack, but raise your arms only part-way) Skip count by 5's as you do.

Xylophone

Let's play the xylophone. Get your mallets and strike out a tune while you skip count by any number.

Xenpos

A xenpos is a small South American bird with a laterally flattened bill. They use their beak to forage for insects in bark or tree stumps. Peck with your beak to find tasty insects as you skip count by any number.

Active Math — Skip Counting

Xiaosaurus

A Xiaosaurus was a small, plant-eating dinosaur that lived during the Jurassic period. Pretend to eat plants as you skip count by any number.

Yacht Racing

Man the rudder and beware the rigging. You are in a yacht race! Skip count by any number as you navigate your way through a narrow channel.

Yellow Cab

You're the driver of a yellow cab. Does your fare need to get there in a hurry? Don't forget to skip count while you drive to their destination.

Yesteryear in Yonkers

The first game of golf ever played in the United States was played in Yonkers in the year 1888. Practice your golf swing while you skip count by any number.

Yo-Yos

On July 27 2008, yo-yoers in Suffolk broke the record for the most people to yo-yo simultaneously with 435 people, only three more than the previous record set two years before. Get out your yo-yo and practice your moves while skip counting by any number.

Active Math — Skip Counting

Zebra

Did you know a zebra's stripes are as unique as human fingerprints? Gallop like a zebra and skip count by any number.

Zero

Stand with your feet together and your arms by your sides. Skip count by any number as you raise your arms into a zero over your head.

Zigzag

Zigzag around the room while you skip count by any number. Be careful not to run into anyone else!

Zip It

Bend at the waist, or at the knees (whatever is most comfortable) to reach the bottom of the zipper and quick! Zip it all the way up to your chin. Skip count by fours as you zip.

sit-down math

Sit-down Math

The Sit-Down Math activities can be incorporated during morning meeting, while sitting on the floor together as a group, or just before a story is read or an active discussion is begun. Many of the activities in this section involve stretching and are intended to be performed quietly. Each number has five movements.

Movements for One-to-One Correspondence

Skip Counting Train

Sit in a circle, cross-legged. One child counts, "one," the next says "two" and on up to twenty, then back down to "one."

Sit-down Math

Crazy Clock

Sit on knees. Move bodies around in clockwise circles. Go around and count "one." Go around and say "two"... continue on to twenty.

Sit-down Math

Snake Slither

Lie on belly and slither to the left "one," slither to the right, "two"... continue on to twenty.

Giraffe Reach

Sit crossed-legged. Reach arms up above head and interlock fingers. Stretch to the left "one," stretch to the right, "two"... continue on to twenty.

Butterfly Wings

Sit on the floor, in butterfly position: soles of the feet together and tucked in so that your legs form wings. Wings up "one," wings down "two"... continue on to twenty.

Sit-down Math

Movements for whisper/loud counting by 2's
Skip Counting Train

Sit in a circle, cross-legged. One child whispers "one" the next says, "TWO!" the next whispers, "three," the next says, "FOUR!"
(continue on to twenty...)

Criss Cross Applesauce for 2's

Sit cross-legged.
Cross arms in front and touch floor "one"
Clap "TWO!"
(continue on to twenty...)

Jack-in-the-Box

Sit in a kneeling position.
Bend down to the floor, whisper "one"
Pop up "TWO!"
(continue on to twenty...)

Caterpillar Catnap

Arms together over-head, hands clasped
Reach up "one"
Bend forward to take a nap "TWO!"
(continue on to twenty...)

Slow Sloth

Lie on back with arms and legs in an upside-down crawling position.
Slowly crawl "one"
Clap "TWO!"
(continue on to twenty...)

Sit-down Math

Movements for whisper/loud counting by 3's
Skip Counting Train

Sit in a circle, cross-legged. One child whispers "one," the next whispers "two," the next says, "THREE!"... continuing on to 30.

Criss Cross Applesauce for 3's

Reach across with left hand to the right "one"
Reach across with right hand to the left "two"
Clap "THREE!"
(continue on to thirty...)

3's Twist

Hands on hips
Twist left "one"
Twist Right "two"
Clap "THREE!"
(continue on to thirty...)

Leopard Leap

Sit on floor with soles of feet together.
Put hands in a pouncing position.
Pounce left "one"
Pounce right "two"
Clap "THREE!"
(continue on to thirty...)

Platypus Plunge

Sit on knees. Make a duck bill by putting the palms of your hands together.
Plunge to the left "one"
Plunge to the right "two"
Clap "THREE!"
(continue on to thirty...)

Sit-down Math

Turtle Twist

Sit on knees
Put hands on hips
Twist left "one"
Twist right "two"
Clap "THREE"
(continue on to thirty...)

Movements for whisper/loud counting by 4's
Skip Counting Train

Sit in a circle, cross-legged. One child whispers "one," the next whispers "two," the next whispers "three," the next says "FOUR!" continuing on to 40.

Criss Cross Applesauce for 4's

Reach out with right hand, touch floor on the left "one"
Reach out with left hand, touch floor on the right "two"
Cross arms over chest "three"
Clap "FOUR!"
(continue on to forty...)

Gorilla Leg Lifts

Sit on the floor with legs straight out in front and knees bent.
Place hands on floor to either side of your body, "one"
Extend right leg "two"
Extend left leg "three"
Clap "FOUR!"
(continue on to forty...)

Sit-down Math

Sailboat Sway

You are a sailboat sailing on a windy day. Put feet in butterfly position and grasp your ankles with your hands.
Sway left "one"
Sway right "two"
Arms up and make a sail, balance yourself "three"
Clap "FOUR!" (continue on to forty...)

Pig Roll

Down on all fours
Roll to the left "one"
Roll to the right "two"
Back up on all 4's "three"
Clap "FOUR!" (continue on to forty...)

Movements for whisper/loud counting by 5's
Skip Counting Train

One child whispers, "one," the next whispers, "two," the next whispers, "three," the next whispers, "four," the next says, "FIVE!" and so on, (continue on to fifty...)

Criss Cross Applesauce for 5's

Reach left with right hand, touch the floor "one"
Reach right with left hand, touch the floor "two"
Touch right knee with left hand "three"
Touch left knee with right hand "four"
Clap "FIVE!" (continue on to fifty...)

Sit-down Math

Feed the Ducks

Sit on knees
Feed ducks to the left "one"
Feed ducks to the right "two"
Feed ducks to the front "three"
Grab some more bread, "four"
Clap "FIVE!" (continue on to fifty...)

Monkey Head Roll

Hug your knees to your chest
Roll head to the left "one"
Roll head forward "two"
Roll head to the right "three"
Roll head back "four"
Clap "FIVE!" (continue on to fifty...)

Seal Head Roll

Sit on knees. Fold hands on lap.
Roll head to the left "one"
Roll head forward "two"
Roll head to the right "three"
Roll head back "four"
Clap "FIVE!" (continue on to fifty...)

Movements for whisper/loud counting by 6's

Skip Counting Train

One child whispers, "one," the next whispers, "two," the next whispers, "three," the next whispers, "four," the next whispers, "five," the next says "SIX!" and so on, continuing on to 60.

Sit-down Math

Criss Cross Applesauce for 6's

Sit cross-legged
Bend over and touch floor in front with left hand crossing to right "one"
Touch floor in front with right hand crossing left "two"
Touch right knee with left hand "three"
Touch left knee with right hand "four"
Cross arms over chest "five"
Clap "SIX!"
(continue on to sixty...)

O Little Playmate

Get a partner and sit facing each other.
Touch back of right hands together "one"
Touch back of left hands together "two"
Clap "three"
Touch right palms together "four"
Touch left palms together "five"
Clap "SIX!"
(continue on to sixty...)

Crocodile Back-Talk

Sit with feet in butterfly position; put hands behind your back
Push up with hands to lift the body slightly.
Roll head to the left "one"
Roll head forward "two"
Roll head to the right "three"
Roll head to the back "four"
Sit up straight "five"
Clap "SIX!"
(continue on to sixty...)

Sit-down Math

Lizard's Tongue

Sit on knees.
Crawl with left hand "one"
Crawl with right hand "two"
Reach towards ceiling with left arm "three"
Reach towards ceiling with right arm "four"
Stick out tongue "five"
Clap "SIX!"
(continue on to sixty…)

Movements for whisper/loud counting by 7's
Skip Counting Train

One child whispers, "one," the next whispers, "two," the next whispers, "three," the next whispers, "four," the next whispers, "five," the next whispers, "six," the next says "SEVEN!" continuing on to 70.

Criss Cross Applesauce for 7's

Sit cross-legged
Bend over and touch floor in front with left hand crossing to right "one"
Touch floor in front with right hand crossing left "two"
Touch right knee with left hand "three"
Touch left knee with right hand "four"
Touch right hip with left hand "five"
Touch left hip with right hand "six"
Clap "SEVEN!"
(continue on to seventy…)

Sit-down Math

The Letter "L" Laughs

Sit on the floor with your legs straight out in front of you
Make the letter "L" with your body by keeping you back straight.
Put hands on your knees.
Lift left leg "one"
Lift right leg "two"
Lift left hand "three"
Lift right hand "four"
Touch right shoulder with left hand "five"
Touch left shoulder with right hand "six"
Clap "SEVEN!"
(continue on to seventy...)

Cheerleader

Sit on knees
Cross left hand over to right hip and shake pom pom "one"
Cross right hand over to left hip and shake pom pom "two"
Cross left hand over to right shoulder and shake pom pom "three"
Cross right hand over to left shoulder and shake pom pom "four"
Cross left hand over to right above head and shake pom pom "five"
Cross right hand over to left above head and shake pom pom "six"
Clap "SEVEN!"
(continue on to seventy...)

Sit-down Math

Butterfly Dance

Sit on the floor
Make butterfly wings with your legs and feet.
Put hands on hips.
Flap butterfly wing to the left "one"
Flap butterfly wing to the right "two"
Twist at waist to the left "three"
Twist at waist to the right "four"
Lift left shoulder "five"
Lift right shoulder "six"
Clap "SEVEN!" (continue on to seventy...)

Movements for whisper/loud counting by 8's

Skip Counting Train

One child whispers, "one," the next whispers, "two," the next whispers, "three," the next whispers, "four," the next whispers, "five," the next whispers, "six," the next whispers, "seven," the next says "EIGHT!" and so on, continuing on to 80.

Criss Cross Applesauce for 8's

Sit cross-legged
Bend over and touch floor in front with left hand crossing to right "one"
Touch floor in front with right hand crossing left "two"
Touch right knee with left hand "three"
Touch left knee with right hand "four"
Touch right hip with left hand "five"
Touch left hip with right hand "six"
Cross arms over chest "seven"
Clap "EIGHT!"
(continue on to eighty...)

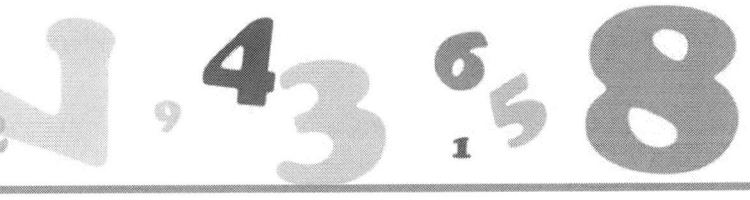

Sit-down Math

Tool Time

Sit on knees
Hammer with left hand "one"
Hammer with right hand "two"
Saw left hand "three"
Saw with right hand "four"
Drill with left hand "five"
Drill with right hand "six"
Cross hands across chest "seven"
Clap "EIGHT!"
(continue on to eighty...)

Terrific Toads

Put feet in frog position.
Put hands on feet, fingers pointing forward and wrists touching ankles.
Put weight on hands so that you are hunched over.
Stretch head to left "one"
Stretch head forward "two"
Stretch head to right "three"
Stretch head back "four"
Stretch head to left and up "five"
Stretch head to right and up "six"
Stick out tongue to catch a bug "seven"
Clap "EIGHT!"
(continue on to eighty...)

Sit-down Math

Sparrow Strut

Sit on the floor
Make wings with your legs and feet.
Put hands on hips.
Flap wing to the left "one"
Flap wing to the right "two"
Twist at waist to the left "three"
Twist at waist to the right "four"
Lift left shoulder "five"
Lift right shoulder "six"
Lift both shoulders "seven"
Clap "EIGHT!" (continue on to eighty...)

Movements for whisper/loud counting by 9's

Skip Counting Train

One child whispers, "one," the next whispers, "two," the next whispers, "three," the next whispers, "four," the next whispers, "five," the next whispers, "six," the next whispers, "seven," the next whispers "eight," the next says "NINE!" and so on to 90.

Criss Cross Applesauce for 9's

Sit cross-legged
Bend over, touch floor with left hand crossing to right "one"
Touch floor in front with right hand crossing left "two"
Touch right knee with left hand "three"
Touch left knee with right hand "four"
Touch right hip with left hand "five"
Touch left hip with right hand "six"
Touch right shoulder with left hand "seven"
Touch left shoulder with right hand "eight"
Clap "NINE!"
(continue on to ninety...)

Sit-down Math

Cheetah Claws

Sit on your knees.
Cross over and sharpen left claw on floor on right "one"
Cross over and sharpen right claw on floor on left "two"
Cross over and sharpen left claw on right thigh "three"
Cross over and sharpen right claw left on thigh "four"
Cross over and sharpen left claw on right tree "five"
Cross over and sharpen right claw on left tree "six"
Cross over and reach up. Sharpen left claw on right tree "seven"
Cross over and reach up. Sharpen right claw on left tree "eight"
Clap "NINE!"
(continue on to ninety...)

Frog Wave

Sit in frog feet position with a straight back.
Put hands on your waist.
Put shoulders back.
Stretch to the left "one"
Stretch forward "two"
Stretch to the right "three"
Stretch back "four"
Put arms straight up in the air.
Stretch to the left "five"
Stretch forward "six"
Stretch to the right "seven"
Stretch back "eight"
Clap "NINE!"
(continue on to ninety...)

Sit-down Math

Butterfly

Make butterfly wings by putting the soles of your feet together.
Put hands on hips.
Flap butterfly wing to the left "one"
Flap butterfly wing to the right "two"
Twist at waist to the left "three"
Twist at waist to the right "four"
Stretch head to left "five"
Stretch head to right "six"
Flap left arm "seven"
Flap right arm "eight"
Clap "NINE!"
(continue on to ninety...)

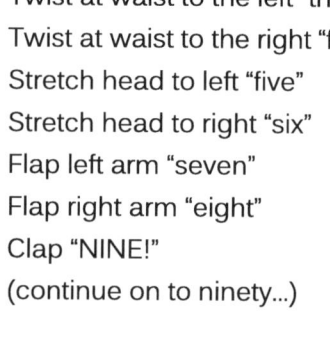

Tapping at the Table

Tapping at the Table movements are designed to be used while children are sitting at their desks. The movements allow the benefits of one-to-one correspondence and practice with counting of multiples while still maintaining a quiet room. They can be used as transitional activities or when a child's brain needs recharging. There are three movements for each number. Children gain in their skill level by counting both forward and backward.

Movements for One-to-One Correspondence

Drum Tapping

Use two fingers to tap the desk like drum sticks. Cross over (right arm to left side of desk, and vice versa) and tap while counting from one to 20 (or higher) forward and backward.

Criss Cross Tap

Gently tap the desk with the palm of your hand while counting from one to 20 (or higher) forward and backward.

Follow the Leader

Make a pattern of taps on different parts of the desk while counting. Have your students imitate the pattern. Allow your students to have a turn being the leader.

Tapping at the Table

Movements for whisper/loud counting by 2's

Drum Tapping

Use two fingers to tap the desk like drum sticks.
Cross arms and tap desk with fingers from both hands "one"
Clap "TWO!"
(continue on to twenty...)

Criss Cross Tap

Cross over and tap the desk with left hand "one"
Clap "TWO!"
Cross over and tap the desk with right hand "three"
Clap "FOUR!"
(continue on to twenty...)

The X's Tap

Cross arms and gently tap the desk with the palm of your hands "one"
Clap "TWO!"
(continue on to twenty...)

Tapping at the Table

Movements for whisper/loud counting by 3's

Drum Tapping

Use two fingers to tap the desk like drum sticks.
Cross over and tap desk with fingers of left hand "one"
Cross over and tap desk with fingers of right hand "two"
Clap "THREE!"
(continue on to thirty...)

Criss Cross Tap

Cross over and tap desk with palm of left hand "one"
Cross over and tap desk with palm of right hand "two"
Clap "THREE!"
(continue on to thirty...)

Dog Treats

Pretend you are at the dinner table and your hungry dog is begging for treats.
Cross left hand over and pretend to feed dog under table "one"
Cross right hand over and pretend to feed dog under table "two"
Clap "THREE!"
(continue on to thirty...)

Tapping at the Table

Movements for whisper/loud counting by 4's

Drum Tapping

Use two fingers as drum sticks to tap the desk.
Cross over and tap left of desk with right fingers "one"
Cross over and tap right of desk with left fingers "two"
Cross arms across chest "three"
Clap "FOUR!"
(continue on to forty...)

Criss Cross Tap

Cross over and tap desk with left palm "one"
Cross over and tap desk with right palm "two"
Cross arms across chest "three"
Clap "FOUR!"
(continue on to forty...)

Feed the Fish

Pretend you are feeding the fish at the lake.
To the left of the desk, pretend to drop a piece of bread in the water "one"
To the front of the desk, pretend to drop a piece of bread in the water "two"
To the right of the desk, pretend to drop a piece of bread in the water "three"
Clap "FOUR!"
(continue on to forty...)

Movements for whisper/loud counting by 5's

Drum Tapping

Use two fingers as drum sticks to tap the desk.
Cross over and tap top left of desk with right fingers "one"
Cross over and tap top right of desk with left fingers "two"
Cross over and tap bottom left of desk with right fingers "three"
Cross over and tap bottom right of desk with left fingers "four"
Clap "FIVE!" (continue on to fifty...)

Criss Cross Tap

Cross over and tap top left of desk with right palm "one"
Cross over and tap top right of desk with left palm "two"
Cross over and tap bottom left of desk with right palm "three"
Cross over and tap bottom right of desk with left palm "four"
Clap "FIVE!" (continue on to fifty...)

Naptime

Pretend your desk is a pillow.
Put your left cheek down on desk "one"
Put your right cheek down on desk "two"
Make a sleepy motion with your hands to the left "three"
Make a sleepy motion with your hands to the right "four"
Clap "FIVE!"
(continue on to fifty...)

Tapping at the Table

Movements for whisper/loud counting by 6's

Drum Tapping

Use two fingers as drum sticks to tap desk.
Cross over and tap top left of desk with right fingers "one"
Cross over and tap top right of desk with left fingers "two"
Cross over and tap bottom left of desk with right fingers "three"
Cross over and tap bottom right of desk with left fingers "four"
Cross arms across chest "five"
Clap "SIX!" (continue on to sixty...)

Criss Cross Tap

Cross over and tap top left of desk with right palm "one"
Cross over and tap top right of desk with left palm "two"
Cross over and tap bottom left of desk with right palm "three"
Cross over and tap bottom right of desk with left palm "four"
Cross arms across chest "five"
Clap "SIX!" (continue on to sixty...)

Silly Smiles

Put hands on hips.
Twist to the left "one", twist to the right "two"
Smile to the left "three", Smile to the right "four"
Cross arms across chest "five"
Clap "SIX!" (continue on to sixty...)

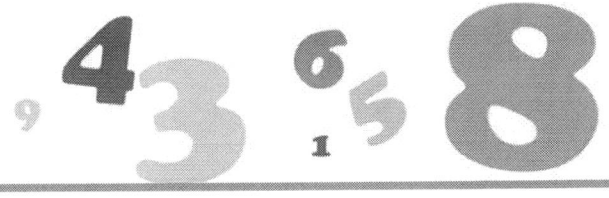

Movements for whisper/loud counting by 7's

Drum Tapping

Use two fingers as drum sticks to tap the desk.
Cross over and tap top left of desk with right fingers "one"
Cross over and tap top right of desk with left fingers "two"
Cross over and tap middle left of desk with right fingers "three"
Cross over and tap middle right of desk with left fingers "four"
Cross over and tap bottom left of desk with right fingers "five"
Cross over and tap bottom right of desk with left fingers "six"
Clap "SEVEN!" (continue on to seventy...)

Criss Cross Tap

Cross over and tap top left of desk with right palm "one"
Cross over and tap top right of desk with left palm "two"
Cross over and tap middle of desk with right palm "three"
Cross over and tap middle of desk with left palm "four"
Cross over and tap bottom left of desk with right palm "five"
Cross over and tap bottom right of desk with left palm "six"
Clap "SEVEN!" (continue on to seventy...)

Pencil Drop

Pretend that you have dropped your pencil!
Reach down to left of desk with right hand to pick up pencil "one"
Reach down to right of desk with left hand to pick up pencil "two"
Put hands on hips. Twist to left "three"
Twist to right "four"
Put arms in air. Stretch to right "five"
Stretch to left "six"
Clap "SEVEN!"
 (continue on to seventy...)

Tapping at the Table

Movements for whisper/loud counting by 8's
Drum Tapping

Use two fingers as drum sticks to tap the desk.
Cross over and tap top left of desk with right fingers "one"
Cross over and tap top right of desk with left fingers "two"
Cross over and tap middle left of desk with right fingers "three"
Cross over and tap middle right of desk with left fingers "four"
Cross over and tap bottom left of desk with right fingers "five"
Cross over and tap bottom right of desk with left fingers "six"
Cross arms across chest "seven"
Clap "EIGHT!"
(continue on to eighty...)

Criss Cross Tap

Cross over and tap top left of desk with palm of right hand "one"
Cross over and tap top right of desk with palm of left hand "two"
Cross over and tap middle of desk with palm of right hand "three"
Cross over and tap middle of desk with palm of left hand "four"
Cross over and tap bottom left of desk with palm of right hand "five"
Cross over and tap bottom right of desk with palm of left hand "six"
Cross arms across chest "seven"
Clap "EIGHT!"
(continue on to eighty...)

Toe Touch

Move chair back from desk far enough that student does not bump his/her head when he/she reaches down to touch toes.
Right hand to left foot "one"
Left hand to right foot "two"
Right hand to left knee "three"
Left hand to right knee "four"
Right hand to left hip "five"
Left hand to right hip "six"
Cross arms over chest "seven"
Clap "EIGHT!"
(continue on to eighty...)

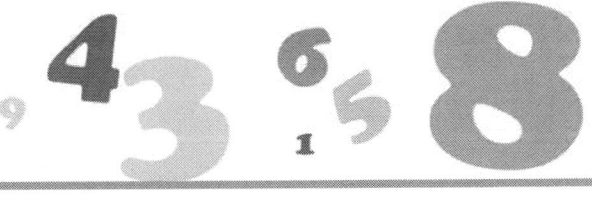

Tapping at the Table

Movements for whisper/loud counting by 9's

Drum Tapping

Use two fingers as drum sticks to tap desk.
Cross over and tap top left of desk with right fingers "one"
Cross over and tap top right of desk with left fingers "two"
Cross over and tap middle left of desk with right fingers "three"
Cross over and tap middle right of desk with left fingers "four"
Cross over and tap bottom left of desk with right fingers "five"
Cross over and tap bottom right of desk with left fingers "six"
Touch left shoulder with right hand "seven"
Touch right shoulder with left hand "eight"
Clap "NINE!" (continue on to ninety...)

Criss Cross Tap

Cross over and tap top left of desk with palm of right hand "one"
Cross over and tap top right of desk with palm of left hand "two"
Cross over and tap middle of desk with palm of right hand "three"
Cross over and tap middle of desk with palm of left hand "four"
Cross over and tap bottom left of desk with palm of right hand "five"
Cross over and tap bottom right of desk with palm of left hand "six"
Touch left shoulder with right hand "seven"
Touch right shoulder with left hand "eight"
Clap "NINE!" (continue on to ninety...)

Macarena

Stretch out left hand, palm down "one"
Stretch out right hand, palm down "two"
Turn left hand palm face up "three"
Turn right hand palm face up "four"
Touch left shoulder with right hand "five"
Touch right shoulder with left hand "six"
Put left hand to the left side of face "seven"
Put right hand to the right side of face "eight"
Clap "NINE!"
(continue on to ninety...)

Hallway Math

Hallway Math movements are designed to be used while children are walking in the hallway from one activity to another. They are intended to be performed quietly where whispered numbers are mouthed and loud numbers are whispered, and clapping is done very quietly with cupped hands. The movements allow for further practice of math during transition times. Have your students practice in the classroom before entering the hallway. Choose one movement and continue with the movement for the entire duration of the transition. Choose a student to be the leader and teacher is the caboose. Once you perfect counting forward, try counting backward. Modify the activity by having the students walk in two lines.

Encourage other classes to compete with your class in the following categories:

- The number of children participating in the activity.
- The level of noise. (The goal is to do the activity without noise.)
- The ability of the class to do the movements simultaneously.
- The level of focused engagement in the activity.

The Hallway Math activities can be modified for different skip counting numbers. Airplane, Cat Scratch, Bunny Hop and Race Car demonstrate how to modify your movements for a variety of skip counting numbers. The Hallway Math activities also work well in the classroom. Continue on to twenty for twos, thirty for threes, and forty for fours, etc.

Hallway Math

The Airplane Movements

Airplane for 2's

Make airplane wings with your arms "one"
Clap "TWO!"

Airplane for 3's

Make airplane wings with your arms straight out
Lift left arm, lower right arm, glide "one"
Lift right arm, lower left arm, glide "two"
Clap "THREE!"

Airplane for 4's

Make airplane wings with your arms straight out
Lift left arm, lower right arm, glide "one"
Lift right arm, lower left arm, glide "two"
Straight arms, glide "three"
Clap "FOUR!"

Hallway Math

The Cat Scratch Movements

Pretend to be kitty cats in need of sharpening your claws.

Cat Scratch for 2's

Scratch with both claws in front of you "one"
Clap "TWO!"

Cat Scratch for 3's

Scratch with left claw "one"
Scratch with right claw "two"
Clap "THREE!"

Cat Scratch for 4's

Scratch with left claw "one"
Scratch with right claw "two"
Scratch with both claws in front of you "three"
Clap "FOUR!"

Hallway Math

The Bunny Hop Movements

Make bunny ears with your hands by placing your hands on forehead (palms forward).

Bunny Hop for 2's

Make bunny ears, "one"
Clap "TWO!"

Bunny Hop for 3's

Make bunny ears.
Bend left ear down (bend left-hand fingers forward) "one"
Bend right ear down (bend right-hand fingers forward) "two"
Clap "THREE!"

Bunny Hop for 4's

Make bunny ears "one"
Bend left ear down (bend left-hand fingers forward) "two"
Bend right ear down (bend right-hand fingers forward) "three"
Clap "FOUR!"

Hallway Math

The Race Car Movements

Pretend to be driving a race car. Put your hands on the pretend steering wheel.

Race Car for 2's

Hold the steering wheel, "one"
Clap "TWO!"

Race Car for 3's

Steer to the left "one"
Steer to the right "two"
Clap "THREE!"

Race Car for 4's

Steer to the left "one"
Steer to the right "two"
Hold steering wheel straight "three"
Clap "FOUR!"

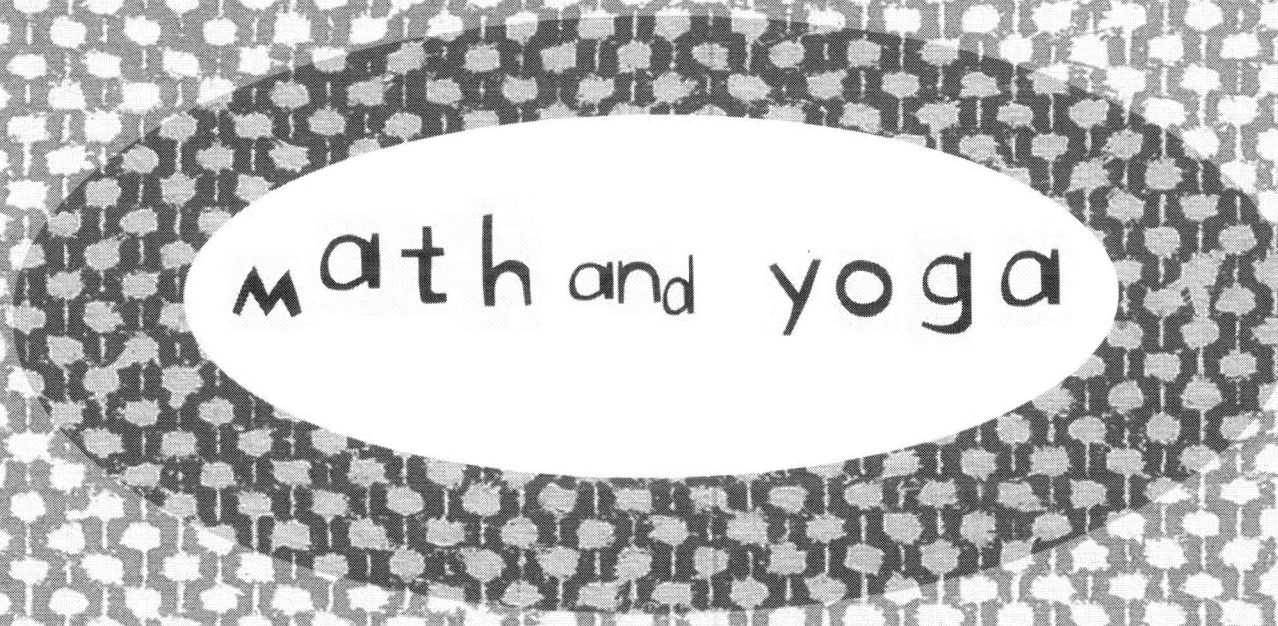

Math and Yoga

Schools are beginning to implement yoga into the curriculum as teachers have found that yoga helps to calm children. It manages their feelings, releases nervous energy, increases self-control and discipline, improves concentration, and enhances learning. The combination of math practice and yoga adds the benefit of helping children to move toward closure with math facts.

Downward Dog

Begin on your hands and knees, legs and arms approximately shoulder width apart
Push upward with your legs and stretch your spine "one"
Lift left hand "two"
Lift right hand "three"
Put knees on floor "four"
Clap "FIVE!"

Math and Yoga

Terrific Triangle

Sit on knees.
Lean back and place hands on floor behind you, fingers facing forward "one"
Stretch belly button up "two"
Sit back on knees "three"
Clap "FOUR!"
(continue on to forty...)

Cat and Dog

Get on all fours "one"
Stretch back upward "two"
Sit on knees "three"
Clap "FOUR!"

Seal Pose

Lie on belly. Place hands flat on floor "one"
Push up with hands and arch back "two"
Lie flat on floor with arms straight forward "three"
Clap (in front of head) "FOUR"

Math and Yoga

Math and the Five Tibetan Rites

The Five Tibetan Rites are an ancient form of yoga that claim to strengthen the body, provide mental clarity, increase circulation, relieve muscular tension and nervous stress, improve respiration and digestion, and to slow aging! These exercises are combined with math practice and will lead to a class of balanced students, eager and ready to tackle new learning. For more information, read the book, *Ancient Secrets of the Fountain of Youth* by Peter Kelder. Search the web for The Five Tibetan Rites for a downloadable pdf file which illustrates the movements.

Rite Number One (Twirling)

Stand facing the wall. Look at one point on the wall. The goal is to have your eyes return to the same point after each twirl.
Twirl clockwise "one"
Twirl again "two"
(continue on to 21...)

Math and Yoga

Rite Number Two (Nose Touch Knees)

Lie on your back with legs straight "one"
Lift head and legs towards each other "TWO!"
(continue on to 42...)

Rite Number Three (Camel's Back)

Kneel "one"
Stretch head back towards floor "TWO!"
(continue on to 42...)

Rite Number Four (Table Top)

Sit with feet facing forward. Hands touching ground, face down "one"
Bend knees with feet flat on the floor. Lift body up and hold "TWO!"
(continue on to 42...)

Rite Number Five (Downward Dog/Seal)

Seal position "one"
Downward Dog position "TWO!"
(continue on to 42...)

activities for the MATH&MOVEMENT® floor mats and banners

Activities for Mats and Banners

The *Math&Movement*™ program is a kinesthetic, multi-sensory approach to teaching math that incorporates physical exercise, stretching, cross-body movements, and yoga activities as covered in this book. As part of the program, I have created a series of visually-pleasing floor mats and banners designed to encourage students to practice math concepts while "moving to the numbers". These mats and banners, as well as desktop charts and other program products, can be used in school classrooms, homeschools and educational enrichment programs. (See our website for more information: www.mathmadefun.com)

The activities in this section of the book relate to specific mats and banners, which are available through the website. They range in level of difficulty; the easier activities are appropriate for pre-K children, the more difficult for grades 4+.

General tip for all mats: Once your students have developed some familiarity with the mats, use a worksheet with problems that can be solved using the mats. Clip the worksheet to a clipboard and let them "move their way to the solutions"! When practicing multiplication, have the child begin with a small number of problems and multiply by only one number. Gradually increase the number of problems on a page. Do not mix multiplication problems until the child has mastered each number.

The Number Line Floor Mat (0-10)
SKU mm0065

The Number Line Floor Mat was designed to help children practice one-to-one correspondence, learn odd and even numbers, practice addition and subtraction and practice counting forward and backwards to ten. One-to-one correspondence is the ability to link a number name with one, and only one, object.

The Number Walk

Take the number walk from zero to ten. As the child steps on each number, encourage the child to simultaneously say the number name.
If the counting gets ahead of the number the child is stepping on, encourage the child to go back and start over. Stepping on the number and saying the number name simultaneously is evidence of a child's understanding of one-to-one correspondence, essential to all mathematical processes. Be sure your student's stepping is in sync with his/her saying the number!

Activities for Mats and Banners

The Number Walk—Backwards

Counting backwards is a prerequisite for subtraction. Encourage your student to start on ten and take steps to zero while saying the numbers!

Buddies

Notice that all the numbers have corresponding dots. This is intended for children to learn the value of the numbers. Notice that the number two has two dots. These two dots are buddies. Two is an even number! The number three has three dots. Two of the dots are buddies but there is one left over! Odd numbers have one left over. Three is an odd number.

Lonely Numbers

Have your students pretend that numbers, like people feel lonely sometimes. Your students can help the numbers not feel lonely by placing objects on the numbers! Place one object on the number one. Place two objects on the number two. Choose two of the same thing—like two shoes, two books, or two toy cars. Place three objects on the number three. Consider choosing three mittens, rocks or spoons. Continue placing objects on the numbers! For bigger numbers like ten, try 10 pennies, paper clips or acorns.

Adding and Subtracting Numbers

Write addition and subtraction problems on cards, and use the Hopping Mat as a number line. If the math problem says 6+3, then stand on 6 and take 3 steps forward to 9! For subtraction problems, walk backwards or count up.

Activities for Mats and Banners

Count-down

Pretend you are on a rocket ready for blast-off. Start on the 10 and count down, 10, 9, 8, 7, ...2, 1, blastoff. Have the child jump up and clap while saying "blast-off!"

Race-to-Ten

Start on zero. Roll one die. Take the number of steps on the die. First one to reach exactly ten wins. If the roll of your die yields a number that causes you to exceed ten go back to zero.

Race-to-One

Start on ten. Roll one die. Take number of steps on the die. First one to reach exactly zero wins. If the roll of your die yields a number that causes you to surpass zero, go back to ten.

Make Ten

Say to child, "Choose a number and then walk to it." Ask child, "How many steps would you have to take to reach ten?" Child figures it out and answers. For example, if child chooses to stand on 6, then answers that it would take 4 steps to reach 10, then adult responds, "yes 6 plus 4 makes 10." If child answers incorrectly, have him or her count again.

Activities for Mats and Banners

Skip Counting Hopping Mats

The Skip Counting Hopping Mats are intended to be used to drill math facts such as addition, subtraction and multiplication. Each mat features a single multiplier (2, 3, 4, 6, 7, 8 or 9) and visually reinforces the multiplier intervals on the number line. For example, the Skip Counting Hopping Mat by 6's has small color blocks for the non-multiple numbers (such as 15 and 22) and large blocks for the multiples (such as 18 and 36). Each mat includes the multiples up to ten times the base multiplier (the 6's mat, for example, goes to 60).

The Skip Counting Hopping Mats are available individually or as a set. The activities described in this section apply to all of the Skio Counting Hopping Mat by X's — just substitute the different multipliers!

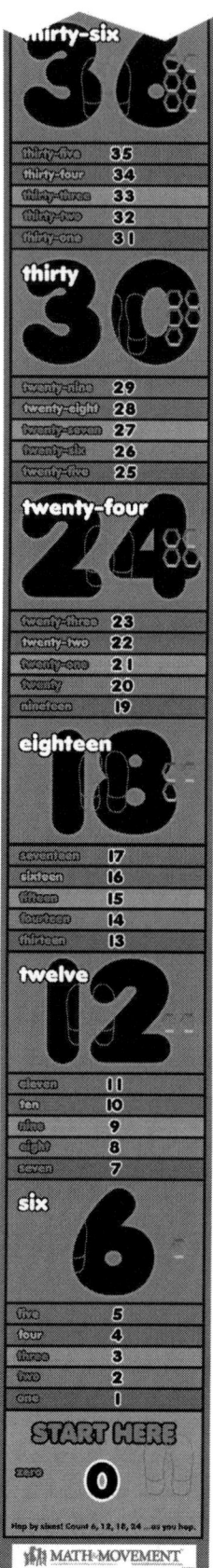

Number Line Hopping Mat by 2's SKU mm0002

Number Line Hopping Mat by 3's SKU mm0003

Number Line Hopping Mat by 4's SKU mm0004

Number Line Hopping Mat by 6's SKU mm0006

Number Line Hopping Mat by 7's SKU mm0007

Number Line Hopping Mat by 8's SKU mm0008

Number Line Hopping Mat by 9's SKU mm0009

The Number Walk

Take the number walk from zero to the end of the mat. See description under Number Line Floor Mat (0-10).

The Number Walk—Backwards

Counting backwards is a prerequisite for subtraction. Encourage the child to start at the end and take steps to zero while saying the numbers!

Lonely Numbers

Play the game Lonely Numbers. See description under Number Line Floor Mat (0-10).

Adding and Subtracting Numbers

Write addition and subtraction problems on cards and use the Hopping Mat as a number line. If the math problem says 8+3, then stand on eight and take three steps forward to eleven! For subtraction problems, walk backwards.

Hopping the Multiples

Learning the multiples is a prerequisite for multiplication. Encourage the child to start on zero and hop the multiples (the large color blocks) while saying the numbers! If the child gets ahead of himself/herself, start over!

Multiplication Mania

Have the child start on zero and hop to the first multipler while saying "one times X is equal to X (substitute the multiplier for X)." Then hop to the next multiplier while saying "two times X is equal to Y (substitute the multiplier for X and the next product for Y)" and so on to the end. Notice that all the multiples have corresponding dots. This is intended for children to learn the value of the numbers and learn that multiplication is addition of groups of items. For example, on the Number Line Hopping Mat by 3's, the number six has six dots to show that six is two groups of three. As the child hops, have him/her use the groups to help say the multiplication problem. Remember, multiplication is fast addition!

Activities for Mats and Banners

Skip Counting Practice

Students line up on either side of the mat. One student hops and the other students chant (count) the multiples as the student hops. Initially, it is common for the student hopping to be out of sync with group chanting of the multiples. If you have a student that likes to hop quickly, encourage him/her to pause on the fifth number. This gives the other students a chance to catch their breath before counting the remaining multiples.

Beginning Factoring

Have one student stand on each multiple. Ask questions of the class relative to the Hopping Mat. For example, if you are working with the Hopping Mat for 6's or the 9's then a question can be who is standing on nine times six? Students can use the pictures on the mat to figure out the answer.
Modifications: To allow the entire class to participate, make teams of two students. Have each pair of students stand on either side of one of the multiples. Depending on the Hopping Mat, ask which team is standing on three times five, eight times seven, or four times six.

Hopscotching the Multiples

Play hopscotch with any of the Hopping Mats. Start at zero. Have the child hop with one foot on the first multiple, then with two feet for the next multiple. The intent is for the student to alternate between one foot, both feet, one foot and then both feet as they hop though the multiples. Encourage students to also begin at the end of the mat and count backwards.

Hopscotching the Multiples with a Multiplication Twist

Make teams of two students. Have one student put a marker on one of the multiples such as a penny, paper clip or acorn. The second student uses the Hopscotching the Multiples activity. When the student comes to multiple with the marker, he/she also says the associated multiplication problem.

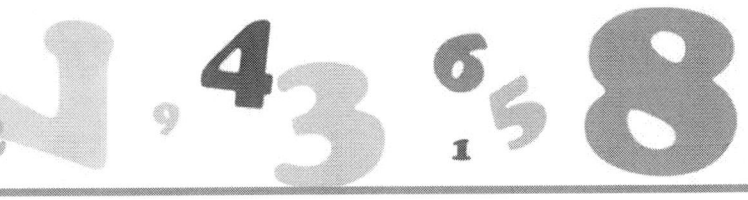

Activities for Mats and Banners

Add/Subtract Classroom Mat
SKU mm0018

Many of the following activities require numbers 1-100 on cards. Write numbers 1-100 on index cards, one number per card. Activities may also require dice with different amounts and +/- dice. Other materials include paper cups, black construction paper, tape, index cards and markers.

Tally Treats

Students count items with tallies. Each student adds up the tallies and stands on the mat on that number.

Naughty Nickels

Place nickels in paper cups. Have enough paper cups for each of your students. The number of nickels can vary in each cup. Students take one paper cup, add up the nickels and stand on the sum on the mat.

Daring Dimes

Place dimes in paper cups. Have enough paper cups for each of your students. The number of dimes can vary in each cup. Students take one paper cup, add up the dimes and stand on the sum on the mat.

Quaint Quarters

Place quarters in paper cups. Have enough paper cups for each of your students. The number of quarters can vary in each cup. Students take one paper cup, add up the quarters and stand on the sum on the mat.

Money Madness

Place some quarters, dimes and nickels in paper cups. Students take one paper cup, add up the coins and stand on the sum on the mat. (Note that you can also find US Money mats at www.mathmadefun.com for further money practice.)

137

Activities for Mats and Banners

Even Eagles

Eagles only like to land on even numbers. Can you find an even number to swoop down and land on?

Odd Owls

Owls only like to land on odd numbers. Can you find an odd number to swoop down and land on?

Simon Says

Play the game Simon Says—examples include Simon Says stand on a multiple of 3, an odd number, a square number, a number of which the digits add to 10, etc.

Double-Digit Diagonal

Can you find the only diagonal where all numbers are double digits? What happens when you add the digits?

The Number Walk

Begin by starting at zero. Add a multiplier (such as 3) and step on that number. Continue throughout the 100 number grid, stepping on the multiples (e.g. 6, 9, 12, 18 etc.). Next take the Number Walk backwards from 100. Afterward, take the Number Walk going forward or backward starting at any number.

Sensational Square Number Stroll

Stroll through the square numbers 1, 4, 9, 16, 25, 36, 49, 64, 81 and 100. Square numbers are 1x1, 2x2, 3x3, etc.

Super Squares

Put black construction paper down on the numbers 1, 2, 11, and 12. This makes a 2x2 square and the square number four. Have students count the four squares to discover that 2x2 is actually 4. Ask "What is the next square number? Who can guess?" Students can find the answer by covering the 3 by 3 square (covering the numbers 1, 2, 3, 11, 12, 13, 21, 22, and 23. Have the children skip count by threes, to discover that 3x3 is nine.

Continue laying down pieces of black construction paper to make additional square numbers.

Stupendous Square Roots

Follow the directions for Super Squares activity. After each square has been created, ask "what is the square root of the square number 4, 9, 16," or whatever square number you are discussing. The square root is the number of rows or columns that make the square number. Ask "Who can figure out the square root of 25, 49, or 81?"

Activities for Mats and Banners

Sieve of Eratosthenes

A prime number is a natural number that is greater than one and only has two factors, one and itself. Use the Sieve of Eratosthenes to find all the prime numbers up to 100.

Stand on the number one. One is special—it is neither prime nor composite.
Step to the number two. This number is prime.
Skip count by twos, covering all the multiples of two with black construction paper.
Move to the next number that is not covered with construction paper (in this case it will be three).
Skip count by threes and cover all the multiples of three with black construction paper.
Continue the same pattern until one hundred.
The numbers not covered in black construction paper are the prime numbers.

Terrific Tens

Write +10, -10, +20, -20, +30, -30, +40, -40, +50, -50, +60, -60, +70, -70, +80, -80, +90, -90 on index cards. Have students stand on mat. Choose a card from deck and call out the number and direction (e.g. +80 is read add 80 or -30 is read subtract 30).

Activities for Mats and Banners

The Dice Decide

Each student chooses a two cards from a pile of numbered cards and chooses one of the numbers to stand on and the number on the other card is where the student is trying to move to. Once the student stands on their number, they hand that card to their teacher. The object of the game is to be the first to move to the number on the card that the student is holding. The acceptable movements are based on the roll of the dice. If a 6 and a 4 are rolled, then the student can choose to add or subtract 6, add or subtract 4, add or subtract the sum, difference, product or quotient of 6 and 4.

The Card Rules

The game is played in pairs. Two cards are drawn from the pile and each student receives one card. The students decide who will stand on the mat and who will give directions. One student stands on the mat on the number that is on his/her card. The other student directs him/her based on the second card but does not reveal the number. The goal is to direct the student on the mat to the second number with directions such as add 2, add 30, subtract 4, or subtract 50. When the student on the mat reaches the new number, the students switch places.

Dicey Days

Each student selects a card with a number from 1-100. All students go to the mat and each student stands on his/her number. Instructor rolls a plus/minus die and a traditional die. The students add to or subtract from their number based on the results of the roll of the dice.

Activities for Mats and Banners

Dicey Doggy Days

Play Dicey Days with a die that goes from 1-10 or 1-20

Make Tens

Have students choose a number to stand on. Ask each child how many steps to make a number with 0 in the ones place. For example, if student is standing on 33, he/she figures out how many steps to make 40.

Barney Bumps

Have one student stand on 1 and another on 100. Have each student carefully step on each number while reciting the number. Barney bumps is the number they are on when they meet mid-way. Is the number at the half-way point? Why or why not? While the students are walking, the other students are guessing what number will be the meeting point.

Crazy Count-down

Students line up at the 100. Each marches on the mat counting down from 100 to 1.

Race-to One Hundred

Players line up at 1. Roll dice. Whoever gets the highest number goes first. First player rolls the dice and takes that number of steps. Second player rolls dice and takes that many steps. If second player lands on the spot of the first player, then the first player goes back to zero. Continue until first person reaches 100.

Activities for Mats and Banners

Race to One

Players line up at 100. Roll dice. Whoever gets the lowest number goes first. First player rolls the dice and takes that number of steps backwards. Second player rolls dice and takes that many steps. If second player lands on the spot of the first player, then the first player goes back to 100. Continue until first person reaches one.

Five in a Row—Tic Tac Toe

(created by Sharon Campos, Newfield Elementary School and her students)

Each student receives 9 items of the same color to mark spots on the Add/Subtract Mat). The winner is the first to get five of their items (markers) in a row vertically, horizontally, or diagonally.

Students roll die to determine who is first. In each turn, student rolls die. If an odd number is rolled then student can place marker on any available odd number. If even, then student places marker on even number. Student strategizes as to whether he/she would like to attempt to get five in a row.
Once student has a plan, he/she places his/her marker on the odd or even number specified by the roll of the die.
The next student tries to create his/her own strategy while simultaneously trying to block other students from realizing their goal of five in a row.

Activities for Mats and Banners

Skip Counting Banners

The purpose of the banners is to demonstrate to students that the skip counting numbers have a pattern and are not random numbers. The highlighted number on the banner displays the multiple and makes it possible for children who don't know the multiples to skip count along with the rest of the class. Banners are available individually or as a set at www.mathmadefun.com

Skip Counting 3's Wall Banner mm0011
Skip Counting 4's Wall Banner mm0012
Skip Counting 6's Wall Banner mm0014
Skip Counting 7's Wall Banner mm0015
Skip Counting 8's Wall Banner mm0016
Skip Counting 9's Wall Banner mm0017

Chanting the Multiples

Encourage your class to recite the multiples. Some students will want to challenge themselves by turning their back to the banner, while others become more engaged when they can use the banner to skip count. Adding some form of cross-body movement while reciting the multiples will speed up student's retention.

Skip Counting Hide and Seek

Hang the skip counting banners in clever spots around the building. Create clues as to the location of the banners. Search the building for a banner, when you find it, skip count by that number.

Hide and Seek Patterns

Ask your students to search for the math patterns on the skip counting banners. Did you know that along the nines' diagonal, the digits add to nine or that by reversing these same digits results in another multiple of 9? The patterns are hiding—can you find some more?

Utilize the Waiting Time

Hang banners in locations where students will wait for PE, art, music or lunch. Students will study the patterns as they wait. Skip counting can be used as a filler activity when there are a few minutes to spare such as waiting for the art or computer teacher to call the students into the class. It only takes ten seconds to recite the multiples!

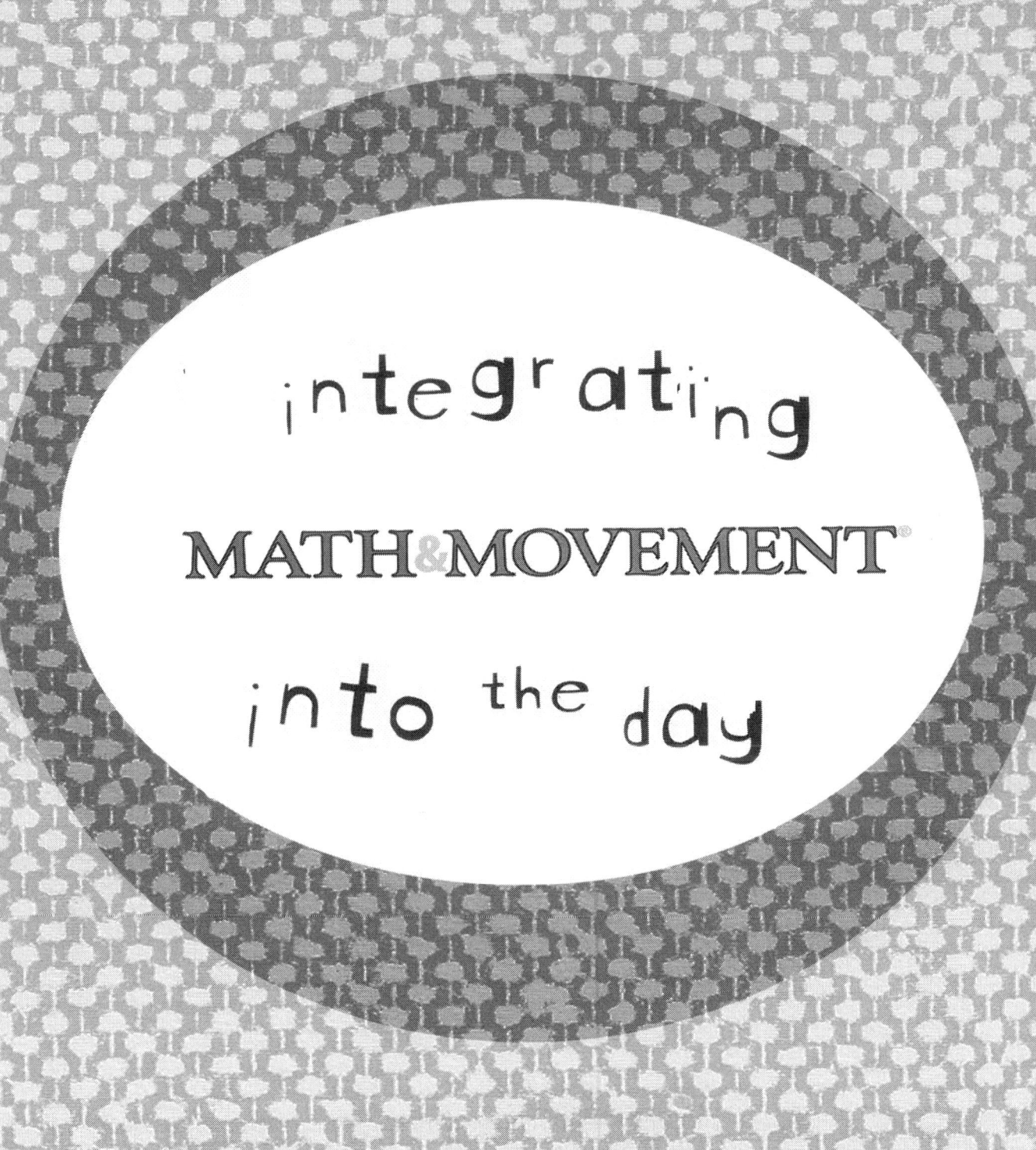

Integrating Math&Movement

Math&Movement activities can be integrated into the regular curriculum by having children recite the multiples after recess, while walking in hallways, waiting in line for lunch, art class or gym, during physical education class, in after-school or to wake up a "sleepy" brain and help to help children process and retain newly learned material. Including the ten seconds that it takes for children to chant the multiples is the most important activity for preparing your students for future success in math. These ten seconds add up quickly and soon your students will be proficient at skip counting. They are then prepared to master multiplication and will be ready to learn division, fractions and factoring. This section will offer suggestions for including *Math&Movement*, describe the steps needed to transfer from skip counting ability to mastery in multiplication, describe how *Math&Movement* can be squeezed into the school day, and offer fifteen suggestions for including additional math practice during the day.

General Suggestions for Integrating *Math&Movement* into the Day

Strive for 5 in the morning and afternoon
Strive for five minutes of *Math&Movement* exercises in the morning and five in the afternoon. More is better and some days allow this but others may not. Encourage your art, music, and PE teachers to join in the fun and begin with a reciting the multiples while skip counting as a warm up activity.

Recognize the Lull
The perfect time to include a *Math&Movement* activity is when there is a lull in the classroom, your students are staring off into space, or you have just said "pay attention" for the third time.

Those who know about the teaching profession recognize the tremendous pressure set on teachers to cover an enormous amount of state-mandated curricula. However, if the teacher continues with the content when the students are not mentally prepared to receive new information, the words are spoken but not received. On the other hand, if the teacher encourages a quick *Math&Movement* break and engages the students in a *Math&Movement* activity, then the students will have a better chance of receiving this new information. So the next time you see that glazed-look or feel the need to say, "Pay

Integrating Math&Movement

attention!" for the fourth time, consider another option. Try saying "Stand up everyone; it's time for the Nine's Twist!" Afterwards, be sure that the children drink plenty of water.

A personal note, as I write this section, I feel myself reaching the point of saturation. I feel that I can't think straight or write another line. Okay—it is time for the Nine's Twist, my personal favorite...90 seconds later, I have just engaged in the Nine's Twist movement from beginning to end, I feel recharged, and I am typing like a maniac!

Advantages to Students of Inventing and Leading Movements Activities

Following are advantages of encouraging your students to create their own *Math&Movement* exercises:

- Children become more engaged in *Math&Movement* activities when they are asked to think of their own activity and lead the class in the activity.

- Giving children the option to suggest and lead movement activities provides leadership and ownership opportunities.

- Children enjoy their classmates' ideas.

- Children can work together in groups thus strengthening their skills in team work.

- When your students lead the activities, you have the opportunity to help other students who may be struggling to coordinate their movements with the counting.

Transferring Skip Counting to Multiplication Mastery

Begin by explaining that multiplication is fast addition of equal groups of items. To demonstrate, lay out counters and organize into groups with the same number in each group. Have your students count the items one at a time. Explain that skip counting is useful for adding the items and demonstrate that four different groups, each with three items can be counted three, six, nine, twelve. The following steps assume that you are learning multiplication by threes. The procedure can be followed for other numbers.

Step One: Introduction
Students pretend to have dots on each of their fingers representing the number of items in their group. Explain that when a student skip counts, it is like they are pretending to add the dots on their fingers. Initially, you can mark each student's fingers with three dots to further explain this concept. Washable markers have worked well for this exercise.

Step Two: Learn how to skip count on your fingers
Have your students stretch out their fingers in front of themselves. Skip count on your fingers by gently squeezing the top of your finger with the thumb and index finger of your other hand. Start with the pinky on your left hand.

Squeeze the top of your pinky and say "3."
Squeeze the top of your ring finger and say "6."
Squeeze the top of your middle finger and say "9."
Squeeze the top of your index finger and say "12."
Squeeze the top of your thumb and say "15."
Switch hands and squeeze the top of your right thumb while saying "18." Count "21, 24, 27 and 30" on your right index, middle, ring finger and pinky, consecutively.

Step 3: Use skip counting on your fingers as a tool for solving multiplication problems.
Skip counting on fingers offers a helpful intermediate step that helps children learn to multiply. Ask your students to multiply 3x3.

151

Have each student hold up three fingers.

Demonstrate by holding up three fingers and emphasize squeezing the top of each finger while simultaneously slowly counting 3, 6, 9.

Another example is solving 4x3. Hold up 4 fingers and skip count by 3's: 3, 6, 9, 12.

Some students will understand the concept immediately and others will need help holding up 4 fingers and using his/her fingers to skip count: 3, 6, 9, 12.

When I have used this method in a classroom, I ask the students to raise their hand when they have the answer. This approach allows me to immediately see which students get the concept and which ones need more assistance. After all the hands are raised, I ask the students to call out the answer. All the students feel successful because the class waits until everyone has the answer.

Please note that counting on fingers is an intermediate step. Once students have learned multiplication, the use of counting on fingers ceases. This method helps to avoid math anxiety because children have a strategy to use to solve the multiplication problem when they can't remember the answer.

Step 4: Moving from skip counting on your fingers to closure in multiplication skills.
There is no substitute for practice, practice and more practice!

···

Math curricula developed since the adoption of the 1989 NCTM's Principles and Standards have shifted the focus from drill and kill to exploration, estimation, problem solving and introduction to a myriad of math concepts that are foreign to those who attended school at an earlier time.

The most noticeable difference in the two approaches is the amount of time allotted to learning basic facts. As someone destined to be a mathematician, I would have benefitted from being introduced to the many math concepts now taught. On the other hand, the modern curricula absolutely do not offer enough practice for most children to reach mastery. My hope is that the *Math&Movement* approach can offer a truce to the math wars.

Integrating Math&Movement

The most successful approach for helping children to reach closure is the continuous combining of physical exercise with skip counting. Mastering multiplication is simple when the skip counting numbers are embedded into your student's memory.

For students who need to learn multiplication but have not yet mastered skip counting, the *Math&Movement* mats and banners can help. Begin by displaying a skip counting banner and asking the students to answer multiplication questions related to the skip counting banner. Looking at the banner allows children to visualize the pattern. Point to the banner and demonstrate the addition of groups. For example, if you are using the skip counting banner by 3's, you might say, "Look at the highlighted numbers. Do you see that they are in groups of three, there are three numbers in the group and the last number is highlighted? Multiplication in this case is the addition of groups of three. Three times three would be adding this group (point to the first group, the number 1, 2 and 3) plus the second group (point to the numbers 4, 5 and 6) and the third group (point to 7, 8 and 9)."

Begin to ask the children multiplication questions. Allow the children to come close to the banner to figure out the answer. Insist that the class waits for everyone to have the answer before calling out the answer. It has worked well to ask children to raise their hand when they have the answer.

Afterward, tape the Hopping mats by 3's in the hallway and have the children hop the multiples of 3's five times. Again ask children multiplication questions and allow them to study the hopping mat to figure out the answer.

Immediately following these activities, have the children practice with multiplication worksheets. Allow children to get up and go to the banner or hopping mat to help them figure out answers.

To transfer from knowledge of skip counting to mastery, begin with math worksheets that have very few problems on a page. Do not mix multiplication problems until children master multiplication by each number. The principal goal in the process is for children to have continuous success. The small number of problems allows for children to feel pride in their accomplishment and confidence from knowing the answer quickly.

Integrating Math&Movement

If a child seems to be agonizing over multiplication problems that they cannot figure out, interrupt the activity and substitute with a worksheet with fewer problems and encourage the child to study the skip counting chart to determine the answer. Agonizing leads to dissatisfaction and frustration in children. These feelings of discouragement and uneasiness with math in elementary school quickly lay the foundation for math anxiety.

It is helpful to begin this multiplication process with 5's and 10's as children generally have an easier time skip counting by these numbers. As a general rule, the very first worksheet should have no more than 12 problems of multiplication by 5's up to 5x5. Before handing the worksheets to the children, practice skip counting by 5's on your fingers. Encourage the children to use their skip counting fingers to figure out the answer.

Gradually increase the level of difficulty of the multiplication questions by increasing the number of questions on each page. In order to provide differentiated instruction, it is encouraged to create a variety of worksheets for your students. Some students will march through the process at a sensational pace and others will seem to be making very slow progress.

My own child, now in the third grade, continues to improve but has by no means reached mastery in her multiplication ability. My now sixth grader, who followed the exact same approach, mastered multiplication at lightning speed. Every child is unique in the time required for them to reach mastery. Is this not the same for learning to read?

Offering a child a calculator in the 4th grade, due to lack of knowledge of multiplication facts, is a disservice beyond measure. There is no substitute for practice of multiplication until each and every child reaches mastery in their multiplication skills.

Fitting *Math&Movement* into an Already Overbooked Day

The *Math&Movement* exercises are designed to embed skip counting into the thinking of young children. Engaging in twelve minutes of *Math&Movement* activities can transform the math ability of your students. But how does one find this extra twelve minutes?

Integrating Math&Movement

The following describes a day where your plan is to introduce and practice skip counting by sixes.

- Include Criss Cross Applesauce in your morning meeting (Takes 1 minute)

- At mid-morning, while children are at their desks and need energizing, do the Tapping at the Table exercise, Criss Cross Tap for 6's. (Takes 1 minute) Please note: The first time I did this activity it took a little longer because one of the students was like a race car speeding through the numbers and out of sync with the rest of the class. The class moaned and glared at the student because I said "We all need to stop and start at the beginning again. It is necessary for all of us, ALL OF US, to count together, perfectly in sync." This individual never raced away again!

- After the Criss Cross Tap for 6's, encourage your students to push their chair back from their desks and count the multiples of 6—only the first five, 6, 12, 18, 24, 30 while they simultaneously cross left elbow to right knee and then right elbow to left knee. Each round takes five seconds; continue for one minute if possible. (Takes 1 minute)

- Go around the room asking each student to recite 6, 12, 18, 24, 30. Listening to their classmates reinforces the numbers. (Takes 2 minutes)

- Develop a Hallway Math move for 6's. For example, have the students cross right hand to left hip, left hand to right hip, then cross right hand to left shoulder, left hand to right shoulder, then touch head with both hands and clap and say 6. Practice in room before taking it to the hallway. (Takes 2 minutes to practice.)

- Choose a leader and use your Hallway Math activity on your next journey out of the classroom. Encourage your students to practice this move until perfection.

- After recess, calm your students with a Math 'n Yoga activity. (Takes 2 minutes.)

- During the mid-afternoon lull, revive your students with the Jaguar Tummy Rub and the 6's Twist (Takes 2 minutes.) Have your students stand at or near their desk to do this activity. Please note that your students may groan at the mention of standing up and exercising but afterwards there will be a marked improvement in their ability to focus and take in more information.

Integrating Math&Movement

At the end of the day, when students have found their belongings and have 4 minutes to wait until dismissal, encourage a student from a higher grade to come into your class and lead a movement for 6's. Encourage the older student to design the move and come prepared to explain the movement. This offers a wonderful leadership opportunity for the older student. It also serves as an impetus to help the "pokey" children to quickly find their belongings and get involved in the activity. See the Math Buddy program for more suggestions. (Takes 1 minute)

At dismissal, march out of the building counting 6, 12, 18, 24, 30 in loud and obnoxious voices. After all, it is the end of the day, hooray!

General Observations

In general, I have noticed that girls seemed to love to pretend to be any type of animal. I have observed them enjoying the movements for Cat Scratch, Pig Roll, Butterflies, Doggy Dig, Three's Dance move and in grades three and above, they enjoyed designing their own dance moves. In addition, I have been able to catch the attention of the boys by pretending to be fishermen casting and reeling, pirates hunting for treasure, dinosaurs stomping, lizards gliding, snakes slithering, or baseball, soccer, football, or hockey players. However, I have been pleasantly surprised that the children willingly participated in their classmates' ideas—even if it was not their interest. I am pleased to report that I have never heard a child say, "that's a dumb idea!"

Frequently Asked Questions and/or Concerns Regarding Math&Movement Activities:

Wild, Out-of-Control Children.
Won't these activities will make them more wild?

The cross-body movements are designed to calm down children rather than get them wilder. However, if a child is wild and out-of-control while engaging in the activity, ask the child to sit down. Also, allow one of your students to lead the activity so you are free to give your attention to the more energetic children. You may choose to solely lead your class in the Tapping at the Table, Sit Down Math or Math 'n Yoga activities until the more energetic children learn the ground rules.

I don't have enough space in my classroom.
The movements can be done while standing at desks or around a small rug. Bring the children outside or to the gym. For my first *Math&Movement* program, I was positive we would need to use a larger space. However, the regular classroom space turned out to be adequate.

We have open classrooms. I don't want to disturb the neighboring classes.
Use the mumble/whisper approach where you whisper the multiples rather than saying or shouting them. Combine with the other classes and do the activities together immediately following recess or at another common time.

Miscellaneous Suggestions for Enhancing Math

My personal belief is that including more math practice stretches your students' thinking and facilitates learning other subjects. Therefore, I encourage you to include math practice as much as possible. Following are some additional suggestions for improving math ability.

Take a *Math&Movement* Quick Break
This activity can be used when the students are sitting at their desks, and a quick *Math&Movement* break will enhance their ability to focus.

> Have the children sit in their chairs making the elephant trunk (see The Elephant March, under Active Math—Whisper/Loud Movements for 3's. (This is also the Brain-Gym Hook-Up position.)
>
> Have right foot cross over left foot, then left foot crosses over right foot, while reciting the multiples.

Math at Recess, Before and After-School
The *Math&Movement* package comes with stencils for painting the Hopping mats by 2's, 3's, 4's, 6's, 7's, 8's, and 9's on the playground, in hallways and on the gym floor. Outside on the playground, consider painting a gigantic hundred number grid, the Cartesian coordinates or a number line that goes from negative 50 to positive 50.

The Seven-Minute Math Work-out
This activity takes seven minutes and consists of the consecutive movements of the 3's Twist, the 4's Twist, the 6's Twist, the 7's Twist, the 8's Twist, and the 9's Twist, without taking a break between the individual movements. Be sure to insist that the children

have plenty of water after completing this work-out. This activity has fit in well after recess, first thing in the morning, or as the very last activity of the day.

Math&Movement Stations

These activities work well for the entire grade-level team or can be modified for an individual class by including less stations. Create stations that incorporate a *Math&Movement* floor mat or banner and define activities associated with these stations. The following example, called Multiplication Marathon, demonstrates stations. Other *Math&Movement* mats such as Add/Subtract mat, Place Value Hop, Cartesian Coordinates and the literacy mats can also be easily incorporated into stations.

Multiplication Marathon

Have children go to the Skip Counting by 3's banner and do jumping jacks while reciting the multiples of three, then go to the Hopping mat by 3's and hop the multiples of three, then grab a clipboard, attach a multiplication by 3's worksheet, and solve the problems. Then go to the Skip Counting by 4's banner and do push-ups while reciting the multiples of four, then go to the Hopping mat by 4's and hop the multiples of four, then grab a clipboard, attach a multiplication by 4's worksheet and solve the problems. To avoid long wait times, have the children begin at different stations. Have mats, banners and worksheets through 9's.

Rainy Day Indoor Recess

Discourage TV on cold or rainy days and replace it with stations in the gymnasium. The stations can be a myriad of math and literacy mats including the Color Hop, The Number Hop, The Blending mats, the Word Hop mats (dolch sight words up to second grade) or the math mats.

School Store

A School Store may be the only time and place that children are allowed to use cash to purchase items, and figure out the change after a purchase. At Newfield Elementary school, the math specialist employs student volunteers to run the school store. Children LOVE the store and flock to it during business hours. It generates revenue and offers children a practical use for their math skills.

Skip Counting Dance Contest

Children seem to enjoy making up their own dances. Divide students into groups. Encourage your students to create dances that incorporate the whisper/loud technique, cross-body movements and clapping on the multiple. Have your groups practice until perfection. Schedule a time when each group can perform their dance. Video tape the dance for any students who are too shy to perform the dance for the class.

Electrical Tape Magic
Recently while at a school, I noticed some electrical tape on the floor. The purpose of the tape was to mark where children should walk down the hall. However, the children had different ideas. I observed the children using the tape as a balance beam. They balanced themselves as they walked along. The activity seemed to enhance balance and coordination.

In the classroom, teachers have found that laying electrical tape in a square around their classroom, marked equidistantly creates an inexpensive number line.

Similarly, using electrical tape to make a number line in the hallways gives children additional math practice. The next activity uses this idea to incorporate positive/negative numbers.

Stepping Out Positive and Negative Numbers
Thirty feet of hallway is required to do this activity. Create a positive/negative number line in the hallway with two 15-foot pieces of yellow (or light-colored) electrical tape. Mark each piece of tape with fifteen equidistant lines, one foot apart. Mark zero in the middle of the two pieces of tape. Write numbers on the number line from one to fifteen and then negative one to negative fifteen.

On separate index cards, write the numbers 0, +1, +2, +3, +4, -1, -2, -3, and -4.

Have your students put their toes on the tape marked "0" and draw out one card from the index cards. Take steps in the direction of the positive or negative sign. For positive numbers move forward, for negative numbers, move backwards. Continue until all cards have been drawn. Afterward, chose two cards, one positive and one negative. Allow your student to process the idea of adding these two numbers by taking steps on the number line.

More Math Homework
Consider sending home a packet of math worksheets and a calendar at the beginning of each month. Ask parents to have child practice 15 minutes a day and sign the calendar that the child has accomplished this task.

Integrating Math&Movement

Counting in the Morning (For Pre-K and K)
Perhaps you have a sign-in routine that asks children to sign their name upon entering the Kindergarten class. Consider a "count-in" routine. Use any of your manipulatives (counters) and have children select one basket of counters to count. After counting, the child writes down the number of items they have counted.

Time to Line Up
Perhaps you have children that fuss over who is first in line. Have you ever heard the complaint "he budged me?" Consider writing the numbers from 1-20 (or number of students in your class) on tongue depressors, popsicle sticks or laminated cards.

When it is time to line up, hand each child one of tongue depressors. The line is formed according to the number on the tongue depressor. I have found that collecting the tongue depressors in order, using a rubber band to keep them organized, allows me to take some out of pile based on the number of students present that day.

Please note that when I looked for tongue depressors at the local craft store, I found that some brands were rough, potentially causing splinters while others were smooth.

Crazy Rainy Days
On rainy days, when the energy in your classroom is about to explode, put the children's enthusiasm to use by hosting a Skip Counting Show. Each child designs his/her own routine to demonstrate Active Math/ Skip counting. Your student may choose to do jumping jacks while skip counting by twos, push-ups while skip counting by fours or put their imagination to work and pretend to be bunnies hopping, cats pouncing, giraffes swaying their necks, or lions roaring as they skip count by the child's favorite multiple . In general, on rainy days, include significantly more *Math&Movement* activities to help keep sanity in the classroom.

Skip Counting in the Sunshine
On a sunny day when kids beg to go outside to have their lesson, sit in a circle and play the "Skip Counting Train." The goal is to make the train go faster and faster. The train moves when each player turns his/her head and recites a skip counting number. For example, when skip counting by fours, the first player turns and looks at the second player and says 4, the second player turns and looks at the third player and says 8, the third player turns to look at the fourth player and says 12, and so on until 40. The faster you say the skip counting numbers, the faster the train moves.

Integrating Math & Movement

Bus Rides- Keep Your Hands to Yourself

Keep your students' minds active and their hands busy by playing "Tapping on the Bus." Instruct your students in the following steps:

> Lean over and touch their right hand to their left toe and whisper "1."
> Lean over and touch their left hand to their right toe and whisper "2."
> Lean over and touch their right hand to their left toe and whisper "3."
> Lean over and touch their left hand to their right toe and whisper "4."
> Clap and say "5!" (Say it loudly.)
> Lean over and touch their right hand to their left toe and whisper "6."
> Lean over and touch their left hand to their right toe and whisper "7."
> Lean over and touch their right hand to their left toe and whisper "8."
> Lean over and touch their left hand to their right toe and whisper "9."
> Clap and say "10!" (Say it loudly.)

Continue using the same pattern until 50. Modify for different numbers.

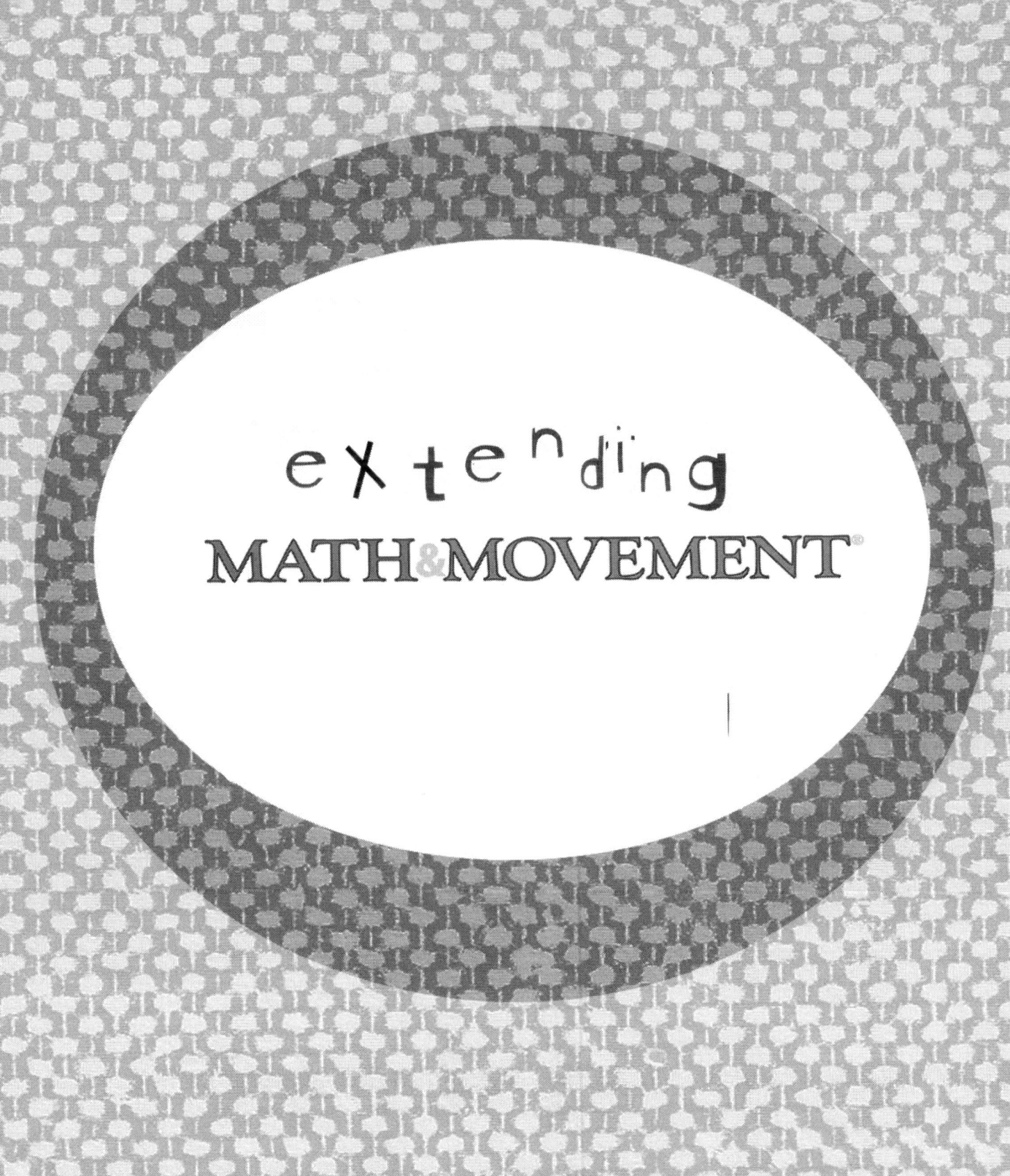

Incorporating movement into your students' school day is only the start! This section includes a variety of suggestions for improving math competence in your community. Some are suggested as fundraisers but are easier to offer without the fundraising component.

Math Buddy Program

The Math Buddy program teams older and younger students for the purpose of enhancing math ability in both groups. The concept for the Math Buddy program is borrowed from the highly successful K-buddy program where an older student improves his/her own reading ability through practice reading. The older student reads to the younger thus getting enjoyable, non-threatening practice with reading. The Math buddy program allows enjoyable, non-threatening math practice for the older student because the older student must fully participate in the activities he/she is using to teach the younger. The enjoyable movement activities included in the Math Buddy program foster positive feelings toward math for all ages.

Many students in our country lack the necessary basic arithmetic skill to fully participate in the problem solving and critical thinking required by state curricula. Students deficient in basic math skills feel hampered during math class and embarrassed at their lack of knowledge just as students feel embarrassed and uncomfortable when they don't know how to read. This deficiency hinders their acquisition of algebra and geometry, increases probability of dropping out of school, and limits opportunities for college as well as career options.

Extending Math & Movement

The Math Buddy program can be structured to meet the interests of your students. It can team high school with middle or elementary students, middle school students with elementary or older and younger elementary school students. The ratio of older students to younger can also vary. The program is highly successful because both groups of students enjoy the play-like activities associated with the floor mats and banners.

In addition, the Math Buddy program:

Offers the younger students the opportunity to strengthen their math skills through enjoyable activities.

Provides the older students the opportunity to improve their own math skills through teaching others. The process of teaching solidifies one's own knowledge.

Allows older students with weak math skills to "save face." No one has to know about their deficiencies.

Offers older students with weak math skills motivation to quickly improve their own skills.

Provides an opportunity for older students to consider becoming a math teacher.Nationally, there is a shortage of math teachers.

Promotes strong community relationships.

Allows an opportunity for the older students to be role models.

Offers both older and younger students the opportunity to have more physical activity during the day.

The United States ranks 23 out of 30 industrialized countries in math scores. It is crucial to increase math ability across the nation. Math Buddy program is a powerful strategy for enhancing math for those students with insufficient math skills.

Math&Movement Family Fun Night

Are you tired of fundraisers that support the candy and gift wrapping industries? Consider an enjoyable, fast-paced, educational experience that will help your students master troublesome math concepts!

The fun night allows parents and children to enjoy active learning together while meandering through a maze of stations. Each station has one floor mat or wall banner that allows children to enjoy learning a math concept.

According to Ron Clark, who taught in Harlem for many years before founding the Ron Clark Academy, "If we want to improve math ability in our students, we need to build an army of tutors." When Clark taught in Harlem, he offered dinner once a week in order to teach the parents how to teach math to their kids. The Math&Movement Family Fun Night is just such an opportunity to teach math concepts to the parents, who can then feel more confident in tutoring their children.

Extending Math&Movement

Parents who participate in the Math&Movement fun night are often amazed the power of Math&Movement to transform their child. They have enjoyed watching their child hopping on the Number Line Hopping Floor Mats to learn the multiples! Parents and children alike have been intrigued by the math patterns that come to life on the giant 100 number grid floor mat (Add/Subtract Floor Mat). Parents hop along with their child around the Clock Hop to learn to tell time. Some parents, who never understood math concepts such as positive and negative numbers, Cartesian coordinates, or fractions, learn the concepts with the mats!

One fundraiser generally provides the funding to purchase the floor mats and banners for the fun night. Afterward, these resources can be used in the regular classroom, in the after-school program, for after-school enrichment classes and for future PTA/PTO/PTSO sponsored fun nights. The Family Fun Night can also be sponsored by your church, school or other organization to provide a free, fun evening of math movement for your community!

A-Penny-A-Problem

A-Penny-A-Problem is a math-a-thon that allows students to increase their math skills and to raise money for their school.

One version of the mechanics of the math-a-thon follows:

The students bring home a pledge sheet one week before the start of the math-a-thon. Students are encouraged to obtain pledges of one penny per problem from parents, grandparents, neighbors or friends.

> Students obtain math worksheets from the school that are appropriate for their academic level. Students are encouraged to solve as many easy problems as possible. Teachers, parents or other volunteer staff will correct math worksheets and tally the total number of points that the child received. The child will receive one point for each correct answer. The child will have the opportunity to correct his/her error(s) to receive full credit.

Extending Math&Movement

The math-a-thon will run for 5 days. Each day of the math-a-thon the principal will report the number of problems solved by each grade level and then by the whole school.

Corporate sponsors can be sought to sponsor the entire school.

A simpler version is to hold a math-a-thon that is not a fundraiser. This version was a gigantic success at an elementary school in New York. The worksheets were displayed on a table outside of the office. Students devoured worksheets like candy and went back to find more. Teachers scrambled to restock the worksheets. The key to the success was the daily announcement made by the principal stating the number of problems that the students had solved. In addition, individual classrooms challenged each other to see who could solve more problems. Following is a description of the event:

The Elementary School students challenged their mental calculators while participating in a PTO sponsored Math-A-Thon during the week of April 23-27. On Monday morning, the principal announced the start of the Math-A-Thon along with the challenge: SOLVE AS MANY MATH PROBLEMS AS YOU CAN THIS WEEK!

The students responded to the challenge in a manner that far exceeded expectations by solving 6,335 math problems in just the first day. The enthusiastic students' desire to solve more and more math problems left parent volunteers and teachers happily scrambling to quickly create more math problems.

The students' smiles were contagious as they brought their solved math problems into the office to put in the Math-A-Thon box. The students solved 15,171, 12,183, and 17,320 math problems on the following days of the Math-A-Thon.

On Friday at 2:45, the announcement of the grand total of 51,129 problems solved caused the children to cheer throughout the school.

At a time when our nation is searching for methods to improve math and science education, Trumansburg elementary has found an innovative technique for making practicing math lots of fun.

Congratulations to the elementary students, faculty and staff!

After School Math Immersion

After school teachers are eager to use their time in productive ways, but they are hampered by the children's need to move around after a day spent in classrooms. Math&Movement's innovative techniques capitalize on the fact that the majority of children are kinesthetic learners. The Math&Movement activities and floor mats allow students to immerse themselves in enjoyable math activities dovetailing their own physical needs. After school practice of math concepts is key to mastery.

In addition, after school programs that have access to the Math&Movement Floor Mats and manipulatives allow their students to complete their homework assignments using a concrete, rather than abstract, approach.

Math 'n Tennis Camp

During our February week-long vacation, a Math 'n Tennis Camp was offered to students in our community. The camp was organized with stations which the students rotated through. The students drilled in tennis strokes and engaged in enjoyable math activities which allowed the students to have "fun with math." Their favorite activity was the creation of gigantic shapes made from toothpicks and mini-marshmallows!

Math 'n Summer Camp

Since research has demonstrated a correlation between physical exercise and learning, I propose combining active learning with summer camp experiences modeled after the Math 'n Tennis Camp. In general, the model is to have children engage in intense physical exercise and then to follow those experiences with learning.

Math Resource Centers

Math resource centers provide support for experiential learning. They offer a home for math manipulatives, science kits, puzzles, math floor mats, reading manipulatives, social studies kits and all types of materials that enhance learning through exploration.

Benjamin Franklin and a group of like minded business associates pooled their money to begin the first lending library in the 1700s. In order for math to flourish, we need to pool our resources and begin math resource centers.

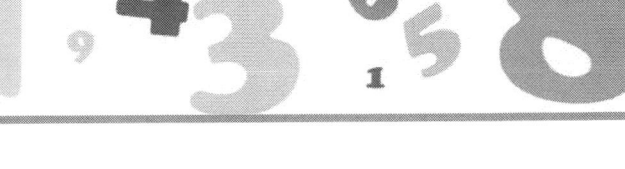

Conclusion

If you could incorporate one new strategy into your daily routine that had the power to transform the lives of your students, enabling them to live confident and competent lives, then would you modify your program to include this strategy?

Inability in math cripples students. After one of my radio interviews, a parent contacted me. She told me the story of her son. He was not good at math and she didn't bother to ensure that he mastered the math concepts. She explained to me that at the time she didn't realize her error. She thought, "Oh well—he just won't be an engineer." However, the reality was that upon entering high school, his self-esteem plummeted. He began telling her that he was stupid because he could not understand math. He doubted his ability to graduate. He repeatedly told her that he was very dumb because he couldn't understand math. After many years of intense encouragement and counseling, he finally did graduate. After listening to the radio interview, she reflected on her own experience. Her conclusion was that her son needed to be competent in math to feel fully confident. "If only I had known this when he was younger!" she exclaimed. "It would have saved us years of aggravation."

The US is a nation at a crossroads. Will we continue to lead the world or will our position be usurped by another nation? By making active learning an integral part of your students' school day, you have the ability to protect and perpetuate the American dream.

In addition, I believe we have the power to reduce and eliminate math illiteracy. We are fortunate to have the example and model of those who have recognized the need for improving literacy and have been successful in doing so. Their techniques can be used to promote numeracy!

For example, illiteracy used to be much more of an issue in my community, but ten years ago a local non-profit agency called the Family Reading Partnership took on the challenge of creating a "culture of literacy" by promoting family reading practices in the community and beyond. A handful of volunteers committed to literacy worked together to promote the importance and the pleasure of reading with one's child. The powerful words "Read to Me" with beautiful artwork featuring families reading to children were enlarged into huge banners and hung on buildings throughout the community. In

Conclusion

addition, the Family Reading Partnership developed programs through which books are given as gifts to families after the birth of a child, at well child doctor's visits, and to welcome children to school at kindergarten registration. An annual Kids' Book Fest was organized and the community was invited to come, free of charge to meet authors and engage in enjoyable literacy activities linked to books. The Family Reading Partnership continues to dream big and pursue creative strategies to weave books and family reading into the fabric of this community.

Brigid Hubberman, the founder of the Family Reading Partnership has inspired me tremendously. By observing her work for community literacy, it helped me to recognize that our world has the same needs for math literacy. The many wonderful programs in place for literacy such as the Summer Reading program, Read-A-Thons or the K-Buddy program could be "tweaked" and borrowed to enhance math literacy. By combining all our efforts and tackling the serious issue of math phobia, math anxiety and math illiteracy we, like the Family Reading Partnership, have the opportunity to do a magnificent deed for our children. My hope in creating this program was to catapult us toward the goal of eradicating all forms of math anxiety and creating a math literate society, with the Math&Movement movements, floor mats and banners as a source of enjoyable learning for your students.

We all know that due to many modern-day factors, children are struggling to learn their math facts. Some may even finish elementary school without mastery of facts. My goal in developing this program was to make math fact mastery possible for children struggling to learn these concepts. My dream is to give <u>every</u> child, regardless of gender, race or socio-economic status, the exciting opportunity to be confident and competent in their math ability and to be able to use their math ability as a tool in any career they pursue. The frequent practice of the Math&Movement activities will not only help your students stay physically fit, but allow mastery, the first step in making this incredible dream possible.

So the next time the intense energy level of your students is about to drive you crazy, put their energy to good use by having them flop down on the floor and do push-ups while skip counting by 3's—all the way to infinity!

Acknowledgements

I am so thankful for all the help from Laura Gates-Lupton and the teachers and students from the classrooms of Northeast Elementary School, South Hill Elementary School, Newfield Elementary School and R.C. Buckley Elementary School. Many of the ideas in the book were the inspiration of the students in these schools. I greatly appreciated the support and help from teachers Margaret Steinacher, Sharon Campos, Phil LInde, Torey Compton, Carol Dentes-Wilhelm, Barbara Alm, Traci Washburn, Rebeccas Porras and Kelly Baughan. I so appreciate the flexibility of my illustrator Chad Hovey! My mother, Mary Lou Dopyera, a retired reading specialist, read and re-read the manuscript and listened to my ideas. I am indebted to her thoughtful contributions and wisdom over the many years that this book was in process. My father and stepmother, John and Margaret Lay-Dopyera, both retired professors in psychology and early childhood education and the authors of the book *Becoming a Teacher of Young Children* (McGraw-Hill College, 1990 4th Edition), offered numerous helpful suggestions, read, proofed and re-read the manuscript. My husband has supported my endeavors from the beginning and helped with the children and household chores giving me the necessary time to complete this book. Through the process of writing this book, my children have mastered the technique of asking me a question while I am absorbed in writing. They ask, take a deep breath and begin to count to ten. If they are lucky, they get an answer before ten! My daughters are my greatest joy. I am so appreciative of their love and support!

About the authors

Suzy Koontz is an educational consultant, an actuary, a math teacher and author. She is the founder of the Math & Movement® Program and is a popular speaker at schools, PTA/O and homeschool events. Suzy lives in Ithaca, New York with her husband and four daughters.

Laura Gates-Lupton is a freelance writer and editor. Her work has appeared in Woman's World, Highlights, Rainbow Rumpus and others. She lives with her family in the hills to the west of Ithaca, NY, and when she can't sleep, she recites her times tables backwards.